THE COMPUTER SECURITY ENHANCEMENT ACT OF 1997 TO AMEND THE NATIONAL INSTITUTE OF STANDARDS AND TECHNOLOGY ACT TO ENHANCE THE ABILITY OF THE NATIONAL INSTITUTE OF STANDARDS AND TECHNOLOGY TO IMPROVE COMPUTER SECURITY, AND FOR OTHER PURPOSES

HEARING

BEFORE THE

COMMITTEE ON SCIENCE
SUBCOMMITTEE ON TECHNOLOGY
U.S. HOUSE OF REPRESENTATIVES

ONE HUNDRED FIFTH CONGRESS

FIRST SESSION

JUNE 19, 1997

[No. 20]

Printed for the use of the Committee on Science

U.S. GOVERNMENT PRINTING OFFICE

44–187CC　　　　WASHINGTON : 1997

For sale by the U.S. Government Printing Office
Superintendent of Documents, Congressional Sales Office, Washington, DC 20402
ISBN 0-16-055882-4

COMMITTEE ON SCIENCE

F. JAMES SENSENBRENNER, JR., Wisconsin, *Chairman*

SHERWOOD L. BOEHLERT, New York
HARRIS W. FAWELL, Illinois
CONSTANCE A. MORELLA, Maryland
CURT WELDON, Pennsylvania
DANA ROHRABACHER, California
STEVEN SCHIFF, New Mexico
JOE BARTON, Texas
KEN CALVERT, California
ROSCOE G. BARTLETT, Maryland
VERNON J. EHLERS, Michigan
DAVE WELDON, Florida
MATT SALMON, Arizona
THOMAS M. DAVIS, Virginia
GIL GUTKNECHT, Minnesota
MARK FOLEY, Florida
THOMAS W. EWING, Illinois
CHARLES W. "CHIP" PICKERING,
  Mississippi
CHRIS CANNON, Utah
KEVIN BRADY, Texas
MERRILL COOK, Utah
PHIL ENGLISH, Pennsylvania
GEORGE R. NETHERCUTT, JR.,
  Washington
TOM A. COBURN, Oklahoma
PETE SESSIONS, Texas

GEORGE E. BROWN, Jr., California RMM*
RALPH M. HALL, Texas
BART GORDON, Tennessee
JAMES A. TRAFICANT, Jr., Ohio
TIM ROEMER, Indiana
ROBERT E. "BUD" CRAMER, Jr., Alabama
JAMES A. BARCIA, Michigan
PAUL MCHALE, Pennsylvania
EDDIE BERNICE JOHNSON, Texas
ALCEE L. HASTINGS, Florida
LYNN N. RIVERS, Michigan
ZOE LOFGREN, California
LLOYD DOGGETT, Texas
MICHAEL F. DOYLE, Pennsylvania
SHEILA JACKSON LEE, Texas
BILL LUTHER, Minnesota
WALTER H. CAPPS, California
DEBBIE STABENOW, Michigan
BOB ETHERIDGE, North Carolina
NICK LAMPSON, Texas
DARLENE HOOLEY, Oregon

TODD R. SCHULTZ, *Chief of Staff*
BARRY C. BERINGER, *Chief Counsel*
PATRICIA S. SCHWARTZ, *Chief Clerk/Administrator*
VIVIAN A. TESSIERI, *Legislative Clerk*
ROBERT E. PALMER, *Democratic Staff Director*

––––––––

SUBCOMMITTEE ON TECHNOLOGY

CONSTANCE A. MORELLA, Maryland, *Chairwoman*

CURT WELDON, Pennsylvania
ROSCOE G. BARTLETT, Maryland
VERNON J. EHLERS, Michigan
THOMAS M. DAVIS, Virginia
GIL GUTKNECHT, Minnesota
THOMAS W. EWING, Illinois
CHRIS CANNON, Utah
KEVIN BRADY, Texas
MERRILL COOK, Utah

BART GORDON, Tennessee
EDDIE BERNICE JOHNSON, Texas
LYNN N. RIVERS, Michigan
DEBBIE STABENOW, Michigan
JAMES A. BARCIA, Michigan
PAUL MCHALE, Pennsylvania
MICHAEL F. DOYLE, Pennsylvania
ELLEN O. TAUSCHER, California

––––––––

*Ranking Minority Member
**Vice Chairman

CONTENTS

APPENDIX

(III)

H.R. 1903—THE COMPUTER SECURITY ENHANCEMENT ACT OF 1997—TO AMEND THE NATIONAL INSTITUTE OF STANDARDS AND TECHNOLOGY ACT TO ENHANCE THE ABILITY OF THE NATIONAL INSTITUTE OF STANDARDS AND TECHNOLOGY TO IMPROVE COMPUTER SECURITY, AND FOR OTHER PURPOSES

THURSDAY, JUNE 19, 1997

U.S. HOUSE OF REPRESENTATIVES,
COMMITTEE ON SCIENCE,
SUBCOMMITTEE ON TECHNOLOGY,
Washington, DC.

The Subcommittee met at 10:47 a.m., in room 2318 of the Rayburn House Office Building, Hon. Constance A. Morella, Chairwoman of the Subcommittee, presiding.

Mrs. MORELLA. I am going to call to order the meeting of the Science Committee, the Subcommittee on Technology.

I thank our panelists for being so patient. We did decide in the vote not to adjourn.

[Laughter.]

Mrs. MORELLA. There was a plan to have a series of other votes, which is why I was delayed and other members of the Subcommittee are delayed. And, they just decided they were going to try to negotiate a problem they have with the rule on the defense bill. And, therefore, we will commence our hearing, which is quite important.

Today's hearing is going to focus on H.R. 1903, the Computer Security Enhancement Act of 1997. I would like to begin by complimenting the Subcommittee's Ranking Member, Bart Gordon, for his hard work in helping craft a bipartisan bill to address our government's computer security needs.

And, along with Mr. Gordon, Science Committee Chairman Sensenbrenner, Ranking Democratic Member Brown, Committee Vice Chair Ehlers, Representatives Davis, Stabenow, Jackson Lee, Sessions, Pickering, Traficant, Cook, Cannon and I have all introduced H.R. 1903. The bill amends and updates the Computer Security Act of 1987, which gave the National Institute of Standards and Technology the lead responsibility for developing security standards and technical guidelines for civilian government agencies' computer security.

Specifically—and I will run down the highlights of the bill—it reduces the cost and improves the availability of computer security technologies for federal agencies by requiring NIST to promote the federal use of off-the-shelf products for meeting civilian agency computer security needs. Second, it enhances the role of the independent Computer System Security and Privacy Advisory Board in NIST's decision-making process. The board, which is made up of representatives from industry, federal agencies and other outside experts, should assist NIST in its development of standards and guidelines for federal systems.

It also requires NIST to develop standardized tests and procedures to evaluate the strength of foreign encryption products. Through such tests and procedures, NIST, with assistance from the private sector, will be able to judge the relative strength of foreign encryption, thereby defusing some of the concerns associated with the export of domestic encryption products.

Fourth, it clarifies that NIST's standards and guidelines are to be used for the acquisition of security technologies for the Federal Government and are not intended as restrictions on the production or use of encryption by the private sector.

The bill also addresses the shortage of university students studying computer security. I find this really remarkable, that of the 5,500 PhD's in computer science awarded over the last 5 years in Canada and the United States, only 16 were in fields related to computer security.

To help address such shortfalls, the bill establishes a new computer science fellowship program for graduate and undergraduate students studying computer security. The bill sets aside $250,000 a year, for each of the next 2 fiscal years, to enable NIST to finance computer security fellowships under an existing NIST grant program.

And, finally, the bill requires the National Research Council to conduct a study to assess the desirability of creating public key infrastructures. The study will also address advances in technology required for public key infrastructure.

You know, all of these measures I have brought out are intended to accomplish two goals. First, to assist NIST in meeting the ever-increasing computer security needs of federal civilian agencies; second, to allow the Federal Government, through NIST, to harness the ingenuity of the private sector to help address its computer security needs.

Since the passage of the Computer Security Act, the networking revolution has improved the ability of federal agencies to process and transfer data. It has also made that same data more vulnerable to corruption and theft.

You know, in February, the General Accounting Office highlighted computer security as a government-wide, high risk issue in its "High Risk Series." GAO specifically identified the lack of adequate security for federal civilian computer systems as a significant problem.

While this is the first time that GAO included computer security in its high risk series, it's not the first time that GAO has addressed this issue. Since June of 1993, the General Accounting Office has issued over 30 reports detailing serious information security weaknesses at federal agencies.

And, in a September 1996 report, GAO reported that over the past 2 years, serious information control weaknesses existed at 10 of the 15 largest federal agencies. The significance of these weaknesses cannot be understated.

According to another GAO report, in 1995 alone, the Department of Defense may have experienced as many as 250,000 attacks to its computer systems. It's estimated that fully 64 percent of these attacks succeeded in gaining access to DOD systems.

Concurrent with the release of GAO's high risk report, this Subcommittee held the second in a series of computer security briefings that I had initiated in the 104th Congress. During the briefing, members of the Science Committee heard from some of the most respected experts in the field. They all agreed that the Federal Government must do more to secure the sensitive electronic data it possesses.

In response, I included increased authorizations, with the approval of this Subcommittee, of $10 million a year in H.R. 1271, the Federal Aviation Administration Research, Engineering and Development Authorization Act of 1997, and $4 million a year in H.R. 1274, which was the NIST Authorization Act of 1997. These increases, if appropriated, should allow the FAA to conduct the research required to improve the security of its computer systems and enable NIST to increase its efforts to improve computer security in federal agencies.

The increase in authorizations, however, is only one part of the solution. Updating the Computer Security Act to enable NIST to better utilize private sector advances in computer security technologies is another.

The Federal Government is not alone in its need to secure electronic information. The corruption of electronic data threatens every sector of our economy.

The market for high quality computer security products is enormous. And, the U.S. software and hardware industries are responding. The passage of H.R. 1903, I believe, will enable the Federal Government, through NIST, to benefit from these technological advances.

I look forward to hearing from our distinguished panelists today. And, in my estimation, it's a good bill. And, I am hopeful we can move it through the legislative process in short order.

And, I am now delighted and honored to recognize the Ranking Member of this Subcommittee for his comments, Mr. Gordon.

[The text of H.R. 1903 follows:]

105TH CONGRESS
· 1ST SESSION

H. R. *1903*

IN THE HOUSE OF REPRESENTATIVES

Mr. SENSENBRENNER (for himself, Mr. BROWN of California, Mrs. MORELLA, Mr. GORDON, Mr. DAVIS of Virginia, Ms. STABENOW, Mr. EHLERS, Ms. JACKSON LEE of Texas, Mr. SESSIONS, ▮▮▮▮▮▮ Mr. PICKERING, Mr. TRAFICANT, and Mr. COOK) introduced the following bill; which was referred to the Committee on _______________________

A BILL

To amend the National Institute of Standards and Technology Act to enhance the ability of the National Institute of Standards and Technology to improve computer security, and for other purposes.

1   *Be it enacted by the Senate and House of Representa-*

2 *tives of the United States of America in Congress assembled,*

3 **SECTION 1. SHORT TITLE.**

4   This Act may be cited as the "Computer Security Enhancement Act of 1997".

5 hancement Act of 1997".

June 16. 1997 (3:41 p.m.)

2

1 SEC. 2. FINDINGS AND PURPOSES.

2   (a) FINDINGS.—The Congress finds the following:

3   (1) The National Institute of Standards and

4   Technology has responsibility for developing stand-

5   ards and guidelines needed to ensure the cost-effec-

6   tive security and privacy of sensitive information in

7   Federal computer systems.

8   (2) The Federal Government has an important

9   role in ensuring the protection of sensitive, but un-

10   classified, information controlled by Federal agen-

11   cies.

12   (3) Technology that is based on the application

13   of cryptography exists and can be readily provided

14   by private sector companies to ensure the confiden-

15   tiality, authenticity, and integrity of information as-

16   sociated with public and private activities.

17   (4) The development and use of encryption

18   technologies should be driven by market forces rath-

19   er than by Government imposed requirements.

20   (5) Federal policy for control of the export of

21   encryption technologies should be determined in

22   light of the public availability of comparable

23   encryption technologies outside of the United States

24   in order to avoid harming the competitiveness of

25   United States computer hardware and software com-

26   panies.

3

1   (b) PURPOSES.—The purposes of this Act are to—

2   (1) reinforce the role of the National Institute

3   of Standards and Technology in ensuring the secu-

4   rity of unclassified information in Federal computer

5   systems;

6   (2) promote technology solutions based on pri-

7   vate sector offerings to protect the security of Fed-

8   eral computer systems; and

9   (3) provide for the assessment of the capabili-

10   ties of information security products incorporating

11   cryptography that are generally available outside the

12   United States.

13 SEC. 3. VOLUNTARY STANDARDS FOR PUBLIC KEY MAN-

14   AGEMENT INFRASTRUCTURE.

15   Section 20(b) of the National Institute of Standards

16 and Technology Act (15 U.S.C. 278g–3(b)) is amended—

17   (1) by redesignating paragraphs (2), (3), (4),

18   and (5) as paragraphs (3), (4), (7), and (8), respec-

19   tively; and

20   (2) by inserting after paragraph (1) the follow-

21   ing new paragraph:

22   "(2) upon request from the private sector, to

23   assist in establishing voluntary interoperable stand-

24   ards, guidelines, and associated methods and tech-

25   niques to facilitate and expedite the establishment of

4

1   non-Federal management infrastructures for public

2   keys that can be used to communicate with and con-

3   duct transactions with the Federal Government;".

4 SEC. 4. SECURITY OF FEDERAL COMPUTERS AND NET-

5   WORKS.

6   Section 20(b) of the National Institute of Standards

7 and Technology Act (15 U.S.C. 278g–3(b)), as amended

8 by section 3 of this Act, is further amended by inserting

9 after paragraph (4), as so redesignated by section 3(1)

10 of this Act, the following new paragraphs:

11   "(5) to provide guidance and assistance to Fed-

12   eral agencies in the protection of interconnected

13   computer systems and to coordinate Federal re-

14   sponse efforts related to unauthorized access to Fed-

15   eral computer systems;

16   "(6) to perform evaluations and tests of—

17   "(A) information technologies to assess se-

18   curity vulnerabilities; and

19   "(B) commercially available security prod-

20   ucts for their suitability for use by Federal

21   agencies for protecting sensitive information in

22   computer systems;".

23 SEC. 5. COMPUTER SECURITY IMPLEMENTATION.

24   Section 20 of the National Institute of Standards and

25 Technology Act (15 U.S.C. 278g–3) is further amended—

5

1   (1) by redesignating subsections (c) and (d) as

2   subsections (f) and (g), respectively; and

3   (2) by inserting after subsection (b) the follow-

4   ing new subsection:

5   "(c) In carrying out subsection (a)(3), the Institute

6 shall—

7   "(1) emphasize the development of technology-

8   neutral policy guidelines for computer security prac-

9   tices by the Federal agencies;

10   "(2) actively promote the use of commercially

11   available products to provide for the security and

12   privacy of sensitive information in Federal computer

13   systems; and

14   "(3) participate in implementations of

15   encryption technologies in order to develop required

16   standards and guidelines for Federal computer sys-

17   tems, including assessing the desirability of and the

18   costs associated with establishing and managing key

19   recovery infrastructures for Federal Government in-

20   formation.".

21 **SEC. 6. COMPUTER SECURITY REVIEW, PUBLIC MEETINGS,**

22   **AND INFORMATION.**

23   Section 20 of the National Institute of Standards and

24 Technology Act (15 U.S.C. 278g–3), as amended by this

25 Act, is further amended by inserting after subsection (c),

6

1 as added by section 5 of this Act, the following new sub-

2 section:

3 "(d)(1) The Institute shall solicit the recommenda-

4 tions of the Computer System Security and Privacy Advi-

5 sory Board, established by section 21, regarding standards

6 and guidelines that are being considered for submittal to

7 the Secretary of Commerce in accordance with subsection

8 (a)(4). No standards or guidelines shall be submitted to

9 the Secretary prior to the receipt by the Institute of the

10 Board's written recommendations. The recommendations

11 of the Board shall accompany standards and guidelines

12 submitted to the Secretary.

13 "(2) There are authorized to be appropriated to the

14 Secretary of Commerce $1,000,000 for fiscal year 1998

15 and $1,030,000 for fiscal year 1999 to enable the Com-

16 puter System Security and Privacy Advisory Board, estab-

17 lished by section 21, to identify emerging issues related

18 to computer security, privacy, and cryptography and to

19 convene public meetings on those subjects, receive presen-

20 tations, and publish reports, digests, and summaries for

21 public distribution on those subjects.".

22 **SEC. 7. EVALUATION OF CAPABILITIES OF FOREIGN**

23 **ENCRYPTION.**

24 Section 20 of the National Institute of Standards and

25 Technology Act (15 U.S.C. 278g–3), as amended by this

7

1 Act, is further amended by inserting after subsection (d),

2 as added by section 6 of this Act, the following new sub-

3 section:

4   "(e)(1) If the Secretary has imposed, or proposes to

5 impose, export restrictions on a product that incorporates

6 encryption technologies, the Institute may accept technical

7 evidence from the commercial provider of the product of-

8 fered to indicate that encryption technologies, embodied

9 in the form of software or hardware, that are offered and

10 generally available outside the United States for use, sale,

11 license, or transfer (whether for consideration or not) pro-

12 vide stronger participation for privacy of computer data

13 and transmissions of information in digital form than the

14 encryption technologies incorporated in the commercial

15 provider's product.

16   "(2) Within 30 days after accepting technical evi-

17 dence from a commercial provider under paragraph (1),

18 the Institute shall evaluate the accuracy and completeness

19 of the technical evidence and transmit to the Secretary,

20 and to the Committee on Science of the House of Rep-

21 resentatives and the Committee on Commerce, Science,

22 and Transportation of the Senate, a report containing the

23 results of that evaluation. The Institute may obtain assist-

24 ance from other Federal and private sector entities in car-

25 rying out evaluations under this paragraph.

8

1 “(3) Not later than 180 days after the date of the
2 enactment of the Computer Security Enhancement Act of
3 1997, the Institute shall develop standard procedures and
4 tests for determining the capabilities of encryption tech-
5 nologies, and shall provide information regarding those
6 procedures and tests to the public.

7 “(4) The Institute may require a commercial provider
8 seeking evaluation under this subsection to follow proce-
9 dures and carry out tests developed by the Institute pursu-
10 ant to paragraph (3).”.

11 **SEC. 8. LIMITATION ON PARTICIPATION IN REQUIRING**
12 **ENCRYPTION STANDARDS.**

13 Section 20 of the National Institute of Standards and
14 Technology Act (15 U.S.C. 278g–3), as amended by this
15 Act, is further amended by adding at the end the following
16 new subsection:

17 “(h) The Institute shall not promulgate, enforce, or
18 otherwise adopt standards, or carry out activities or poli-
19 cies, for the Federal establishment of encryption standards
20 required for use in computer systems other than Federal
21 Government computer systems.”.

22 **SEC. 9. MISCELLANEOUS AMENDMENTS.**

23 Section 20 of the National Institute of Standards and
24 Technology Act (15 U.S.C. 278g–3), as amended by this
25 Act, is further amended—

 1   (1) in subsection (b)(8), as so redesignated by

 2   section 3(1) of this Act, by inserting "to the extent

 3   that such coordination will improve computer secu-

 4   rity and to the extent necessary for improving such

 5   security for Federal computer systems" after "Man-

 6   agement and Budget)";

 7   (2) in subsection (f), as so redesignated by sec-

 8   tion 5(1) of this Act, by striking "shall draw upon"

 9   and inserting in lieu thereof "may draw upon";

10   (3) in subsection (f)(2), as so redesignated by

11   section 5(1) of this Act, by striking "(b)(5)" and in-

12   serting in lieu thereof "(b)(8)"; and

13   (4) in subsection (g)(1)(B)(i), as so redesig-

14   nated by section 5(1) of this Act, by inserting "and

15   computer networks" after "computers".

16 **SEC. 10. FEDERAL COMPUTER SYSTEM SECURITY TRAIN-**

17   **ING.**

18   Section 5(b) of the Computer Security Act of 1987

19 (40 U.S.C. 759 note) is amended—

20   (1) by striking "and" at the end of paragraph

21   (1);

22   (2) by striking the period at the end of para-

23   graph (2) and inserting in lieu thereof "; and"; and

24   (3) by adding at the end the following new

25   paragraph:

10

1   "(3) to include emphasis on protecting sensitive

2   information in Federal databases and Federal com-

3   puter sites that are accessible through public net-

4   works.".

5 **SEC. 11. COMPUTER SECURITY FELLOWSHIP PROGRAM.**

6   There are authorized to be appropriated to the Sec-

7 retary of Commerce $250,000 for fiscal year 1998 and

8 $250,000 for fiscal year 1999 for the Director of the Na-

9 tional Institute of Standards and Technology for fellow-

10 ships, subject to the provisions of section 18 of the Na-

11 tional Institute of Standards and Technology Act (15

12 U.S.C. 278g–1), to support students at institutions of

13 higher learning in computer security. Amounts authorized

14 by this section shall not be subject to the percentage limi-

15 tation stated in such section 18.

16 **SEC. 12. STUDY OF PUBLIC KEY INFRASTRUCTURE BY THE**

17   **NATIONAL RESEARCH COUNCIL.**

18   (a) REVIEW BY NATIONAL RESEARCH COUNCIL.—

19 Not later than 90 days after the date of the enactment

20 of this Act, the Secretary of Commerce shall enter into

21 a contract with the National Research Council of the Na-

22 tional Academy of Sciences to conduct a study of public

23 key infrastructures for use by individuals, businesses, and

24 government.

11

1   (b) CONTENTS.—The study referred to in subsection

2 (a) shall—

3   (1) assess technology needed to support public

4   key infrastructures;

5   (2) assess current public and private plans for

6   the deployment of public key infrastructures;

7   (3) assess interoperability, scalability, and in-

8   tegrity of private and public entities that are ele-

9   ments of public key infrastructures;

10   (4) make recommendations for Federal legisla-

11   tion and other Federal actions required to ensure

12   the national feasibility and utility of public key in-

13   frastructures; and

14   (5) address such other matters as the National

15   Research Council considers relevant to the issue of

16   public key infrastructure.

17   (c) INTERAGENCY COOPERATION WITH STUDY.—All

18 agencies of the Federal Government shall cooperate fully

19 with the National Research Council in its activities in car-

20 rying out the study under this section, including access

21 by properly cleared individuals to classified information if

22 necessary.

23   (d) REPORT.—Not later than 18 months after the

24 date of the enactment of this Act, the Secretary of Com-

25 merce shall transmit to the Committee on Science of the

12

1 House of Representatives and the Committee on Com-

2 merce, Science, and Transportation of the Senate a report

3 setting forth the findings, conclusions, and recommenda-

4 tions of the National Research Council for public policy

5 related to public key infrastructures for use by individuals,

6 businesses, and government. Such report shall be submit-

7 ted in unclassified form.

8 (e) AUTHORIZATION OF APPROPRIATIONS.—There

9 are authorized to be appropriated to the Secretary of Com-

10 merce $450,000 for fiscal year 1998, to remain available

11 until expended, for carrying out this section.

12 **SEC. 13. SOURCE OF AUTHORIZATIONS.**

13 Amounts authorized to be appropriated by this Act

14 shall be derived from amounts authorized under the Na-

15 tional Institute of Standards and Technology Authoriza-

16 tion Act of 1997.

Mr. GORDON. Thank you. I want to join Chairwoman Morella in welcoming everyone to this hearing.

Not a day goes by that we don't see some reference in the news to the Internet and the explosive growth of electronic commerce. What was originally envisioned as a network for defense communications and university research is now an international communications network of which we are just beginning to realize its potential.

Both the Office of Technology Assessment and National Research Council reports have identified a major obstacle to the growth of electronic commerce—the lack of widespread use of encryption products. The Computer Security Enhancement Act of 1997 is the first step to encourage the use of encryption products, both by the federal agencies and the private sector. This is, in turn—or, this in turn will support the growth of electronic commerce.

The Computer Security Enhancement Act of 1997, which amends the Computer Security Act of 1987, depends on the close collaboration and cooperation between the National Institute of Standards and Technology and industry in developing standard reference materials and reference standards that are key to commerce. This legislation highlights the need for NIST to expand its activities in the area of electronic commerce.

H.R. 1903 strengthens NIST's role in coordinating federal agencies' efforts to utilize encryption and digital identification products. It encourages federal agencies to adopt and use commercially available encryption technologies whenever possible.

In addition, this legislation allows NIST to evaluate the technical merit of industry claims of the strength of generally available foreign encryption products. Hopefully, this will defuse some of the tension surrounding the issue of export of domestic encryption products.

Not only is this legislation consistent with the recommendations of the Office of Technology Assessment and the National Research Council, it is also in line with a set of resolutions adopted by the NIST Computer System Security and Privacy Advisory Board on June 6, 1997. Finally, I believe this bill is consistent with the goals of President Clinton's upcoming policy announcement on electronic commerce.

I believe that the most important underlying element of H.R. 1903 is that it recognizes that government and private sector computer security needs are similar. Hopefully, the result will be lower cost and better security for everyone.

It has been a pleasure working with Chairwoman Morella on crafting this piece of legislation. I look forward to working with her to move this bill through the legislative process.

I want to thank our witnesses for taking the time to appear before us. And, I look forward to hearing your comments.

Mrs. MORELLA. Thanks, Mr. Gordon. I want to recognize Mr. Brady from Texas, who is here. Do you have any opening comments that you would like to make?

Mr. BRADY. No, thank you.

Mrs. MORELLA. Ms. Rivers from Michigan.

Ms. RIVERS. No, thank you.

Mrs. MORELLA. All right. And, Mr. Ehlers from Michigan also.

Mr. EHLERS. Thank you, Madam Chairwoman. Just a few words. I apologize for being late, but I was—interestingly enough, I was at a meeting with the Speaker and several members on the encryption problem, export encryption problem, and had a very fruitful discussion.

I think very few people realize the importance of computer security and the importance of proper encryption of data flowing over the Internet and other public means of communications. And, I am very pleased that we have this hearing.

I am pleased with your interest in the topic, Madam Chairwoman. And, I am pleased we are taking action on this.

I think it's extremely important for our Nation to be ahead of the curve on this. And, I hope we can soon change—even though that's not directly the concern here, I hope we can soon change our national export policy on encryption so that we can continue to maintain the lead on this issue and can show the rest of the world how it should be done.

Thank you very much.

Mrs. MORELLA. Thank you, Mr. Ehlers. I am glad you were at that meeting.

And, I note also—in my opening comments, I indicated that you are also a co-sponsor of this legislation we are considering.

And, now on to hear the distinguished panel that we have. Thank you, again, first of all, for your patience. You found out what it's like to testify here in the House of Representatives. I am sure that the Senate is probably not even as timely as we are.

I would like to just recognize—and we will proceed in this order, probably asking you to speak maybe not more than about 5 minutes, knowing that your total testimonies will be included in the record; so, if you want to, abbreviate—the Honorable Gary Bachula, the Acting Under Secretary for Technology in the Technology Administration of the U.S. Department of Commerce; Mr. Whitfield Diffie, who has his doctorate in technical sciences, distinguished engineer, Sun Microsystems from Mountain View, California, welcome; Mr. Stephen Walker, who is the President and CEO of Trusted Information Systems, Incorporated, Glenwood, Maryland; Mr. James Bidzos, President and CEO of RSA Data Security, Redwood City, California, thank you for being here; and, Marc Rotenberg, Director, Electronic Privacy Information Center, Washington, DC., Esquire, thank you also.

I appreciate it. And, we will start off then with Mr. Bachula.

STATEMENT OF HON. GARY R. BACHULA, ACTING UNDER SECRETARY OF COMMERCE FOR TECHNOLOGY, U.S. DEPARTMENT OF COMMERCE TECHNOLOGY ADMINISTRATION, WASHINGTON, DC

Mr. BACHULA. Thank you, Madam Chairwoman, for the opportunity to testify on H.R. 1903, the Computer Security Enhancement Act of 1997.

I, first, want to commend you and the Committee members and your staff for turning the attention of Congress to the vital issue of securing our government's and our Nation's information infrastructure. I do have a longer written statement which I would like to be included in the record and with your permission, I would offer some highlights in my oral testimony.

Mrs. MORELLA. With no objection, that will be the case.

Mr. BACHULA. Madam Chairwoman, we stand today at the dawn of a whole new world of electronic commerce, doing business digitally using the emerging information infrastructure. This new era will change all of our lives.

It will allow businesses to buy and sell, to recruit workers, make contracts, exchange money and to organize instantaneous supply chains around the globe. It will allow consumers a dizzying set of choices in banking, making travel reservations, home shopping and literally, will eventually, allow them to custom order products where hitting the return button on home PC will start in motion a process of custom designed assembly of materials, manufacturing and shipping that may occur in only a day or two.

Within a few years, you may be able to order a custom made suit fit to your exact measurements from a highly interactive electronic catalog that will allow you to see the suit on a model, maybe even a model of yourself, turn it around to three dimensions, allow you to try different styles, colors or fabrics before your eyes. And, then when you order that suit, you will set in motion a process where fabric will be shipped from a supplier in one State to a factory in another. Very high tech cutting machines will assemble that piece of clothing, and the suit will be delivered to your home in just a few days.

And, the system that ordered that suit will arrange for the payment, keep a record so you can order another. And, maybe it will send you a note a year or two later with a discount coupon asking whether you are ready for another one.

Or, imagine shopping for furniture and with the appropriate computer program trying out different pieces and styles of furniture in a very realistic but virtual representation of your own family room. If you like a particular couch, but need it to be 3 inches shorter to fit between your tables, you can make that request as well as test the look of different colors and styles.

And, again, when you order, you will set in motion a whole set of activities that some call manufacturing on demand. Others of us might just call that pretty cool.

But, electronic commerce, to grow and succeed to that kind of vision, requires a reliable, secure and trustworthy environment. To buy and sell over the network, we need to have confidence that I am who I say I am.

We need to have confidence in the integrity of some kinds of information, that some information has not and cannot be tampered with by hackers. We need to know that we can transact business perhaps with our doctors that is private.

We need to have access to public information, but also the assurance that the wrong people will not have access to classified or private information. The tools that make electronic commerce possible are the tools that we are talking about here today.

The discussions can get pretty detailed and esoteric. Sometimes the debates get passionate.

I am not a computer expert myself nor have I engaged in some of these emotional debates. I am here today to talk about NIST's role in computer security and enabling this exciting, rapidly evolving and potentially very lucrative for the U.S. economy, arena of electronic commerce.

When the Computer Security Act was enacted 10 years ago, things were a lot simpler, particularly in the Federal Government. On the whole, our computer systems were centralized; networks were isolated; applications were compartmentalized.

Physical threats to systems were the predominant concern at that time. The term "virus" was just beginning to become part of our lexicon. And, things like digital warfare or digital terrorism were very abstract notions.

Today, government agencies are increasingly delivering services and information directly to citizens via powerful computer applications, using technology that spans the range from large systems to desktop and laptop computers often connected in decentralized networks. These applications are increasingly interactive.

An individual virtually anywhere in the world can access government systems. In many cases, it is the kind of access that the government wants to encourage and should be providing. In other cases, unfortunately, it is not.

In this emerging global information infrastructure, government and private sector systems and networks are increasingly intertwined and, thus, face common threats and risks. Government must be keenly aware that the public is sensitive to issues of electronic access to confidential information, as demonstrated in complaints over access to social security benefits records on line.

Both government and private sectors recognize that the reliability of systems depends upon assurances of personal privacy. Both sectors also have similar requirements for confidentiality, integrity of data and access to public information.

In this rapidly changing environment, the Department of Commerce has and will continue to work with the information technology security framework established by the Executive Office of Management and Budget. OMB recently revised the basic management structure that agency computer security programs should establish, and it identifies specific supporting roles for NIST and other agencies.

NIST's primary responsibility in this area is to provide specific technical standards and guidance to assist federal agencies in meeting their security responsibilities. It's important to remember that it's each agency's responsibility to protect their systems and network, but OMB has provided a common management framework to do that and NIST provides technical guidance and standards.

And, we have played a central role in computer security for the U.S. government long before the passage of the Computer Security Act of 1987. Federal Information Processing Standards called by the acronym in government, FIPS, have provided a common basis for cost effective and reliable information technology and security for government.

By and large, in the development of these standards for federal agencies, NIST references and builds upon the standards developed in the private sector. Today, the government will use such industry-developed standards more and more with NIST participating fully in the voluntary standards process.

I would like to highlight a number of important initiatives that NIST is currently undertaking that we believe will make significant contributions toward more effective computer security practices. First, in the past year, we have reorganized and refocused our information technology activities, consolidating them in a new information technology laboratory. Computer security plays a significant and key role in this new organizational structure.

Mr. BRADY. Mr. Under Secretary, if I may interrupt for a moment, we have reserved another minute for your remarks.

Mr. BACHULA. Another minute? Okay. Thank you. NIST has put out standard—or has put out a request for comments on a new advanced encryption standard. We are looking for comments on additional algorithms in the areas of digital signatures, looking at new technologies to include with the existing ones.

We are very much engaged in an effort to look at a new FIPS in the area of key agreement or exchange protocols. The bottom line is that we are doing a great deal to both provide cutting edge, new technologies and to assist federal agencies to comply with the security requirements that they have.

With respect to the proposed Computer Security Act, again, I applaud the Committee for its leadership. We support many of the provisions of this bill.

We strongly support and applaud the portions of the bill that enable NIST to assist, upon request from the private sector, in the establishment of non-federal public key management infrastructures. We support the provisions relating to NIST providing guidance and assistance to federal agencies, including evaluations and tests of commercially available security technologies.

We support Section 5, which provides that NIST will emphasize technology-neutral policy guidelines and must actively promote commercially available products for meeting the security and privacy requirements of federal agencies.

With respect to Section 6 and Section 8, we support the intent and principles behind those. We think that we need to find some improved language because of some possibilities of misunderstandings about that intent.

The one section of the bill that we must oppose, that the Administration must oppose, is Section 7, which provides for NIST to assess the availability and strength of foreign available cryptographic technology as they relate to export restrictions on encryption. The inclusion of these regulatory provisions in this bill clouds the bill's stated objective of improving the security of Federal Government systems.

It injects a debate into this room that probably belongs somewhere else. Moreover, current law and procedures already establish a government-wide process for making such evaluations.

Under current export control law, foreign availability evaluations are appropriately considered as one of many factors that bear on determinations of export control policy, including the area of encryption technologies.

The proposed section would put NIST, a non-regulatory agency, square in the middle of second-guessing both existing regulatory processes and existing executive branch determinations. Our plea to this Committee is to let NIST do what it does best and not throw us in the middle of this regulatory debate.

We support this bill. We would like to work with the Committee on a couple of language improvements in two sections.

Section 7 causes us a problem. But, by and large, this is a good piece of legislation and we very much applaud the Committee for its efforts.

[The prepared statement of Mr. Bachula follows:]

Prepared Statement of

Gary R. Bachula

Acting Under Secretary of Commerce

for Technology

Before the Subcommittee on Technology

of the House Committee on Science

H.R. 1903

"Computer Security Enhancement Act of 1997"

June 19, 1997

Thank you Madame Chairwoman for the opportunity to testify today on your recently introduced legislation, H.R. 1903, the "Computer Security Enhancement Act of 1997".

I commend you, the Committee members, and your staff for turning the attention of Congress to the vital issue of securing our government's and our Nation's information systems. Almost weekly, it seems, we are confronted with new and mounting examples of risks -- both technological and human -- that undermine public confidence and trust in reliable computer systems and access to information.

When the Computer Security Act was enacted ten years ago, the model for assessing the risk and threat to government information systems seemed simpler. On the whole, federal government computer systems had been centralized, networks were isolated, and applications were compartmentalized. Physical threats to systems were the predominant concern -- the term "virus" was just beginning to become part of our lexicon and "digital warfare" was a very abstract notion.

Today, with the revolution of electronic commerce under way, government agencies are increasingly delivering services and information directly to citizens via powerful applications computers -- utilizing technology that spans the range from large systems to desktop and laptop computers, often connected in decentralized networks. These applications are increasingly interactive. An individual virtually anywhere in the world can access government systems. In many cases, it is the kind of access that the government wants to encourage and should be providing. In other cases, unfortunately it is not.

In the emerging global information infrastructure, government and private sector systems and networks are increasingly intertwined, and thus face common threats and risks. As the Commission on Protecting and Reducing Government Secrecy noted in its recent report, "[J]ust as in the private sector, many federal agencies are reluctant to make the investments required in this area [of computer security] because of limited budgets, lack of direction and prioritization from senior officials, and general ignorance of the threat."

An integrated global network is emerging, with appropriate infrastructure elements to support the growth in global electronic commerce. By utilizing this infrastructure, the government must be keenly aware that the public is sensitive to issues of electronic access to confidential information, as demonstrated in complaints over access to Social Security electronic benefits records on-line. Both sectors recognize that the reliability of systems depends on assurances of personal

privacy. Both sectors also have similar requirements for
confidentiality, integrity and availability of computer systems
and access to public information.

FEDERAL GOVERNMENT COMPUTER SECURITY INITIATIVES

The Federal Government recognizes this technology trend and
is articulating effective information technology policies and
practices in this rapidly changing environment. The Department
has and will continue to work closely with the President's Office
of Management and Budget, which issues management guidance for
information technology in general and information technology
security in particular. I want to call to the Committee's
attention that OMB has recently updated a management framework
for IT security -- consistent across all agencies -- through
Appendix III to its Circular A-130. This revision reflects the
dramatic changes taking place in information technology and its
applications in the Federal Government. Appendix III outlines the
basic management structure that agency computer security programs
should establish, and it identifies specific supporting roles for
NIST and other agencies. NIST's primary responsibility in this
area is to provide specific technical standards and guidance to
assist agencies in meeting their security responsibilities. Thus,
while it is each agency's responsibility to protect their systems
and networks, OMB has provided a common management framework, and
NIST provides technical guidance and standards.

NIST COMPUTER SECURITY ROLE

Long before passage of the Computer Security Act of 1987,
NIST played a central role in computer security for the US
Government. Federal Information Processing Standards (FIPS)
issued by the Department and developed by NIST have provided a
common basis for cost-effective and reliable information
technology and IT security for government. On the whole, FIPS
have referenced and built upon standards developed in the private
sector. Today, the Government will use such industry-developed
standards predominantly, with NIST participating fully in the
voluntary standards process.

NEW INITIATIVES TO MEET THE CHALLENGES

Within the current NIST budget provided for computer
security activities, and recognizing that no one agency can solve
all of the challenges that are posed in the area of computer
security, we are establishing priorities to meet federal
government customer needs and reaffirm our long-standing role of
working with the private sector. Let me highlight for the

Committee a number of these important initiatives that the
Department of Commerce, working through NIST, has undertaken as
significant contributions toward more effective computer security
practices.

First, NIST has in the last year reorganized and refocused
its overall information technology activities to serve better its
internal needs and those of its government and private sector
customers. Computer security continues to play a significant and
key role in this new organizational structure.

In the specific area of IT security, NIST has followed a
strategy recognizing the essentially common security needs of
government agencies and the private sector. We believe that the
best way to provide security for Federal Government systems is to
make maximum use of commercial products, services, standards and
technology. NIST works with the private sector to foster the
availability of security products that may be used by both
government and private sector organizations -- thus achieving
higher levels of security and interoperability for both. The NIST
IT security program focuses on those technologies and needed
infrastructures that will achieve these goals. Briefly, the key
technology focus areas in the NIST IT security program are the
following:
* **Cryptographic Technology and Applications** - to ensure the
    availability of high-quality cryptographic technology
    and application program interfaces to that technology.
* **Public Key Infrastructure** - to ensure interoperability
    and security of the crucial components of the public key
    infrastructure needed to support electronic commerce and
    government activities.
* **Security Criteria and Testing** - to provide objective
    criteria for testing and assessing the functionality and
    assurance of security technology and products.
* **Internet and Network Security** - to provide interoperable
    security capabilities across networks and user "domains".
* **Security Management** - to provide guidance for agencies in
    the selection, implementation and use of security
    technology in their systems and networks.

SPECIFIC COMPUTER SECURITY INITIATIVES AND ACHIEVEMENTS

The Department, again through NIST, has undertaken a number
of significant initiatives designed to increase the security
capabilities of both Federal agencies and private sector
organizations.

NIST is currently seeking public involvement on several
proposed Federal Information Processing Standards which will

further strong computer security through the development and application of important technologies arising out the private sector.

Advanced Encryption Standard. In January of this year, NIST announced that it would begin the process of working with the private sector on an Advanced Encryption Standard (AES). As this Committee knows, the Data Encryption Standard (DES) has been the operative private sector standard, as well as formal government standard, for assuring the confidentiality of information for almost two decades. DES will continue to provide adequate levels of security for many applications for years to come. In an effort to look ahead, NIST has begun the work with the private sector on AES in anticipation that demand for the next generation of encryption standards will require a concerted, multi-year effort to evaluate, develop and build consensus towards acceptable long-term standards. We are pleased by the response of the private sector to this initiative, both at a preliminary workshop this spring and through the positive and significant contributions made to date as suggested inputs in this area.

Expanded Digital Signature Standard. NIST also has requested public comments on additional algorithms that the federal government may endorse to authenticate electronic information and transactions and assure high levels of integrity. This initiative will expand the number of techniques that the Federal government should be using in the area of "digital signatures" and should bring forth the best and most cost-effective technologies that the private sector has to offer. I want to note that we have specifically asked for comment on elliptic curve technology and on RSA's digital signature technology.

Key Agreement or Exchange. In a third area, we have also sought public comments on potential technologies that assure very secure "key agreement or exchange" protocols as part of public cryptographic systems. There is no existing FIPS in this area, and we have specifically asked for comments on the following technologies: RSA, elliptic curve, and Diffie-Hellman.

FedCIRC. The Federal Computer Incident Response Capability (FedCIRC), an initiative originated by NIST and made operational in October 1996, substantially addresses the need in the Federal Government for modern network incident response capabilities. FedCIRC provides, under NIST auspices and in collaboration with DOE's Computer Incident and Advisory Capability and Carnegie-Mellon University's Computer Emergency Response Center (CERT), a variety of subscription funded services such as site evaluation, incident handling services, access to incident and vulnerability advisories, tools and incident repositories and training

opportunities.   Thanks to startup funding from the Government
Information Technology Services initiatives, we are able to
provide 7-day-a-week, 24-hour-a-day service. To date, we have
handled more than 75 incidents from the civil side of government
since we became operational. Additionally, we have fielded
hundreds of other requests for information and assistance. We
have held about 6 workshops and seminars on computer security
since FedCIRC was started.

Public Key Infrastructure. NIST has recently completed
initial work in the area of public key infrastructure by
developing, with the assistance of ten cooperative research and
development agreement partners, a Minimum Interoperability
Specification for Public Key Infrastructure Components (MISPC).
NIST is continuing this work with development of reference
implementations of public key Certificate Authorities and related
technical development.

Army Corp of Engineers Electronic Signature Project. NIST
staff recently received a commendation from the General
Accounting Office for work with the Army Corps of Engineers to
design and implement a procurement system providing for
electronic authentication of transactions.

NIST has also undertaken a long list of activities with
federal agencies designed to improve agency security management,
education and awareness, and use of security technology. NIST
staff would be happy to discuss this with you further.

REVIEW OF THE COMPUTER SECURITY ACT

As the challenges to the security and integrity of
information systems have mounted, both public and private sector
efforts have sought to look at the effectiveness of the Computer
Security Act of 1987, and determine whether any changes should be
proposed.

Most recently, the Department's Computer System Security and
Privacy Advisory Board undertook an effort to solicit views both
from the private sector and from government users on this
question. The Department wants to commend Dr. Willis Ware, Chair
of the Advisory Board, and all the Board members for their hard
work in soliciting a wide variety of views and giving thoughtful
consideration to what changes were needed to the Act and NIST
priorities.

One of the major themes that emerged from this review -- a
theme that underlies the Board's recommendations -- is that

civilian agencies have clearly stated that they need additional
computer security guidance. They are also looking for assistance
in the evaluation, selection, and implementation of computer
products, systems, and applications in order to enhance the
economy and efficiency of computer systems security and private
in the Federal government.

It is notable that after thorough review, the Board did not
recommend any changes in the Computer Security Act of 1987 at
this time. The Board did make two recommendations for NIST to
consider in establishing its priorities.

First, NIST should elevate its commitment to implementing
the Computer Security Act by increasing its assistance to the
civilian Federal agencies. The Board noted that greater
managerial focus and resources should address current computer
security and privacy issues, including greater emphasis on
today's managerial and administrative aspects. The Board noted
high priority items for NIST to address, including acting as a
"central service within the Federal government to advise on the
selection, integration, and use of products and procedures for
securing non-classified systems" and providing "a computer
systems security assessment capability for civilian Federal
agencies". The Board also urged NIST to "maintain a repository
and act as a clearing house for information, techniques,
guidelines and consultation to aid proper use of security
features available in government-used commercial off-the-shelf
software." The Board also urged NIST to "identify exemplary
activities with Federal agencies that can be used as models and
proof-of-concepts for secure civilian government systems". I
note for the Committee that NIST's current Computer Security
Resource Center on the world-wide web addresses many of these
suggestions.

Second, the Board defined a new activity for NIST to
undertake. It specifically recommended that "information should
be gathered about security events and vulnerabilities which exist
in Federal computer systems" and NIST should "develop a
repository for the compilation of this data". In making this
recommendation, the Board noted that "it is imperative that
certain aspects of this information be protected from disclosure"
-- so as to avoid becoming a "cookbook" for potential attackers -
- but that it would be useful to develop a mechanism to report
and track progress in these areas for each civilian Federal
agency and for the promotion of overall security. NIST's FedCIRC
activity, which I mentioned earlier, has this task as one of its
objectives.

The Department is reviewing these recommendations, and will
consider them in light of existing budgets and our role in

working cooperatively with the private sector. The Department also wants to ensure that the appropriate balance is struck between dealing with "today's crises" and strategically preparing for future federal government computer security requirements.

PROPOSED LEGISLATION

I would like to offer my preliminary comments on the newly introduced, H.R. 1903. We have reviewed the bill as reflected in the June 6th "Discussion Draft". Let me again recognize the leadership of this Committee for taking a hard look at the vital issue of computer security, and for proposing changes to the Computer Security Act embodied in the "Computer Security Enhancement Act of 1997". We very much appreciate your effort and commitment to reinforcing the role of the Department, and especially NIST, in its work to promote strong computer security principles, both in government and in the emerging system of global electronic commerce that will be vital for our nation's long-term economic prosperity.

A number of the provisions are consistent with the recommendations produced by the Advisory Board, and NIST's long-standing role in working with the private sector in developing and implementing voluntary standards, guidelines, and conformity assessment practices and techniques.

Let me offer some suggestions which we hope you will consider to several of the bill's sections which we believe are consistent with the right direction that the Committee has outlined.

First, Section 6, as currently written, would require NIST to solicit the recommendation of the Computer System Security and Privacy Advisory Board before submitting a proposed FIPS to the Secretary, and to submit the Board's recommendation along with the recommendation to the Secretary. We agree with the intent of this Section, and would be happy to work with the Committee to develop language that would enable NIST and the Board to continue to work together in a timely and productive fashion.

Second, Section 8, "Limitation on Participation in Requiring Encryption Standards", would prohibit NIST from "promulgating, enforcing, or otherwise adopting standards for use in computer systems other than the Federal government's systems". Since NIST does not develop or issue any standards that are intended for private sector compliance, nor does NIST have any authority to impose standards on the private sector, we are concerned that this language might be misunderstood to preclude NIST from collaborating with the private sector. Again, we would be happy to work with the Committee to develop more appropriate language.

Third, Section 11 establishes a computer security fellowship program with specified levels of funding. NIST, in its continuing efforts to recruit, train, and retain top-notch computer security experts, is keenly aware of the need for increased attention to the IT security research and the training of individuals to conduct such research. We, therefore, believe that Federal Government support of this critical area is important. We strongly support your efforts to provide for computer security fellowships in institutions of higher learning. We believe that computer security education should be supported at all levels of education, from undergraduate to postgraduate, and that there is a need for more degree programs in the discipline of information technology security. In carrying out this activity, we would want to consult with the National Science Foundation, which has the lead in graduate study and training in this area.

The Department looks forward to working with the Committee and accomplishing our mutual goals of strengthening the role of NIST in the area of computer security.

Let me now turn to Section 7 of the proposed legislation. The Administration objects to the inclusion of Section 7, which provides for NIST to assess the availability and strength of foreign-available cryptographic technology as they relate to export restrictions on encryption. The inclusion of these essentially regulatory provisions in this bill clouds the bill's stated objective of improving the security of Federal Government systems. Moreover, current law and procedures already establish a government-wide process for making such evaluations. Under current export control law, foreign availability evaluations are appropriately considered as one of many factors that bear on determinations of export control policy, including the area of encryption technologies. As President Clinton determined in Executive Order 13026, the export of encryption products "could harm national security and foreign policy interests even where comparable products are or appear to be available from sources outside the United States." The proposed section would inappropriately put NIST, a non-regulatory agency, in the position of second guessing both existing regulatory processes and existing executive branch determinations.

CONCLUSION

Thank you, Madame Chairwoman and members of the Committee
for your leadership and for reinforcing the important role of the
Department, through NIST, in promoting security computer systems
and practices. The complexities of global electronic commerce
are becoming a daily part of the work of government, as the
public demands better and more effective services and wider
access to information. We look forward to working with you as
the "Computer Security Enhancement Act of 1997" progresses.

I will be glad to take any questions from the Committee.

GARY R. BACHULA
DEPUTY UNDER SECRETARY FOR TECHNOLOGY

Dr. Mary L. Good resigned as Under Secretary for Technology effective June 3, 1997. Gary R. Bachula (Deputy Under Secretary) is currently the Acting Under Secretary for Technology.

Gary Bachula is the Deputy Under Secretary for Technology at the U.S. Department of Commerce's Technology Administration. As Deputy to Dr. Mary L. Good, the Under Secretary for Technology, Bachula helps to oversee the work of the Office of Technology Policy, the National Institute of Standards and Technology, and the National Technical Information Service.

The Office of the Under Secretary also provides advice and assistance to the Secretary of Commerce for the formulation of new policies and program initiatives for science and technology policy matters. In this capacity, the Technology Administration assists in the development and promotion of Federal technology policies to increase U.S. commercial and industrial innovation, productivity, and economic growth.

Bachula serves as the Department of Commerce representative to the Committee on Education and Training of the National Science and Technology Council.

With both a B.A. in economics and a law degree (J.D.) from Harvard, Bachula served as Chief of Staff to U.S. Rep. Bob Traxler of Michigan from 1974 to 1986, where he advised the Congressman on appropriations for NASA, EPA, the National Science Foundation, and other federal agencies.

From 1986 to 1990 he worked for Michigan Governor James J. Blanchard, serving as Chairman of the Governor's Cabinet Council. The focus of the Cabinet Council was to "reinvent" Michigan's job training and education programs.

Bachula also served as Vice President for Planning and Program Development for CIESIN, the Consortium for International Earth Science Information Network. CIESIN is federally-funded project to intergrate and extend the value of current and future U.S. enviornmental data collection efforts (satellite and on the ground) to a broad array of applied users.

A native of Saginaw, Michigan, Bachula is a 1964 graduate of Saginaw High School, was named Saginaw High's Distinguished Alumnus in 1990. He served at the Pentagon in the U.S. Army during the Vietnam war.

Mr. BRADY. Thank you, Mr. Under Secretary. I know that after the panel concludes, there will be some members of the Committee that will want to talk to you more about Section 7.

Mr. BACHULA. Sure.

Mr. BRADY. Thank you. Dr. Diffie.

STATEMENT OF WHITFIELD DIFFIE, DISTINGUISHED ENGINEER, SUN MICROSYSTEMS, MOUNTAIN VIEW, CA

Mr. DIFFIE. Thank you very much. I would like to thank the Committee for inviting me.

I am going to turn from looking at the future of computer security to looking at the history of how we got to the position we are in at the moment. As I sat down to make these remarks, I realized that NIST and I have been in the cryptographic business for almost exactly the same length of time. It's 25 years ago this coming August that an event I think is worth taking note of occurred.

Larry Roberts, who was the funder of the Arpanet, approached Howard Rosenbloom, who was either Deputy Director for Security or Deputy Director for Research at the time at NSA, and asked for help in development of security technology for the Arpanet. But, he didn't want the work to be classified and they couldn't agree. And, nothing further between those two agencies happened at that moment.

But, Larry Roberts turned and began talking to other people about the security problems of the network. And, one of them was my boss, John McArthy. And, John McArthy, in turn, talked to me.

And, effectively, from the fall of 1972 on, I was working full time in cryptography, having turned from previously theoretical work in computer science. At about the same time, the Bureau of Standards was soliciting for algorithms for what eventually became Federal Information Processing Standard 46, the data encryption standard.

And, although when that was proposed we argued a good deal about its adequacy then—and I was one of the big arguers—I have to admit that it has served very well for the past 25 years. We are much better off with it than without it.

And, the work that we did in developing public key cryptography at Stanford has complemented the development, cryptographic developments at the Bureau of Standards. And, the two things have been used together in the development of appropriate commercial protection systems over this past generation. Now, that was the 1970's.

And, NSA cooperated at that time—and I think it was a genuine cooperation—in the development of the data encryption standard. It appeared that by the early 1980's, they may have had second thoughts about this, having a cryptographic system that was out of their direct control in the way they had been used to.

And, in rapid succession, there was a national security decision directive that would vastly have expanded the authority of DOD over security arrangements throughout the Federal Government. There was a plan by NSA called the "Commercial COMSEC Endorsement Plan" to produce for the first time sort of directly under NSA's imprimatur and by its standard technique—that is, using secret cryptographic systems that would be protected in tamper resistant hardware—to have what was called "Type II" cryptography for the protection of government unclassified sensitive information and all commercial and other information.

And, they would effectively, had that succeeded, have recaptured control over cryptography in the United States. Congress did not consider that appropriate.

It was the subject of widespread protests by industry, particularly the banking community which saw that it needed a much freer, much more openly developed technology. And, in 1987, Congress passed the Computer Security Act, which gave authority to the Department of Commerce, and particularly to the—at approximately the same time renamed—National Institute of Standards and Technology for authority over computer security, network security, communications security standards for civilian government communications.

But, that Act had provisions in it for the NIST to consult with NSA. And, those became expanded into a Memorandum of Understanding between the two agencies that effectively gave NSA control over NIST's actions.

This is a natural outgrowth of having given the authority one way and the money the other way. NIST did not have the resources necessary to do, independently, the work that had been assigned to it.

And, under that regime, which I would trace as running from, let's say, 1989 until some time in the early 1990's, we saw the development and promulgation of three federal information processing standards of which only one, I think, has been generally acclaimed by the outside community. Those were a digital signature standard, developed—incidentally, two out of three of these were developed using academic technology. But, they were developed at NSA.

A digital signature standard, which was not the one which had become a de facto industry standard, and although at a technical level there are pros and cons to each one of those, the effect was opposite to the intent of standardization. It created a rift. It was an attempt to displace an existing standard. And, so far, it has achieved only modest success.

Something more technical called the "secure hash algorithm." That, based on work done at MIT, but elaborated at NSA. And, in general, that has been well received.

And, the most bizarre of the three, the Escrowed Encryption Standard or Clipper Chip, whose strangest feature, to my mind, is that it's a Department of Commerce standard that is based on secret technology that is legally and physically under the control of the Department of Defense and its contractors. So, although the Department of Commerce has legally promulgated the standard, that standard could be cut out from under it by Department of Defense action.

Just incidentally, I spent yesterday at the Armed Forces Communications Electronics exhibition, which is going on here in Washington. And, the government and industry people over there all seem to believe that this technology is about to be declassified.

The NSA people said they tried to get it done in time for the show and didn't succeed. But, maybe the situation is going to be regularized.

Now, I'm very pleased to say that quite recently NIST has begun to take actions that I think are much more consistent with the spirit of the Computer Security Act. They have promulgated a—begun the development of the so-called Advanced Encryption Standard, the replacement for the existing Data Encryption Standard, and done so—I mean, I think Webster said in the last century that the debate couldn't have gone better if his opponent had, you know, planned it that way.

I have to admit that they have followed a course which is very much the course I would have recommended. They began by asking for comments on proposed criteria against which a new standard should be judged.

They declared that the standard would be open, the standard would be unclassified. They are encouraging the submitters to explain everything about the standard, the proposals that they can.

And, I believe this is what is necessary in the modern world in order to have a cryptographic technology that will suit the needs of the diverse community that gives us the promise of this glorious future of Internet commerce and generally a vast improvement in communications that the technology promises.

The diversity of network communications is not measured in the thousands of miles across what the network is or in the millions of machines that are connected to it. It is measured in the diversity of authority, of purposes, of ownership of the devises connected to the network.

And, in order to have security in that environment, which is similar to what we've had all through history—you have to have security in commercial environments; people have to protect goods; they have to assure orders; they have to keep certain secrets—we need a technology that is openly developed and, therefore, can be trusted by everybody who uses it. So, I am very, very pleased to find this legislation, which seems to me to speak to the independence of NIST in performing to this task, to speak to the resources that it needs in performing this task, and I think this bill has come at exactly the right time to support and encourage NIST in what seems to be a return to the, as I would call it, spirit of the Computer Security Act of 1987.

Thank you.

[The prepared statement of Mr. Diffie follows:]

Comments on:
The Computer Security Enhancement Act of 1997

Dr. Whitfield Diffie
Distinguished Engineer, Security

Sun Microsystems

before

The House Science Committee, Subcommittee on Technology

19 June 1997

I would like to begin by thanking Chairwoman Constance A. Morella and
the Committee for inviting me here to comment on the Computer Security
Enhancement Act of 1997. It is a pleasure, for the second time in a
year, to be testifying in favor of something, rather than against it.
It is not only wonderful, but timely, that Congress should be acting to
support NIST's role in the development of computer security standards.

The importance of computer and communication security for the
civilian world first came to light in the early 1970s, in response
to increasing computer use within both industry and government. The
response of what was then the National Bureau of Standards, working in
what appears to have been true cooperation with the National Security
Agency, was to develop a publicly defined cryptographic system for use
in most unclassified applications of the U.S. Government.

By the early 1980s, it appears that some of the NSA participants in
the development of DES, must have had second thoughts. In
September 1984, the President issued National Security Decision
Directive 145, which established a federal policy on safeguarding
'sensitive, but unclassified' information. This directive gave NSA
substantial authority over security policy throughout the Federal
Government and its contractors.

In pursuit of NSDD-145, NSA launched a major program to expand the
use of secure communication facilities in both the public and
private sectors. It announced an ambitious new 'product line,' which
it called 'Type II' in contrast to the Type I equipment used to protect
classified information. As originally conceived, Type II equipment
would be made widely available in the U.S. It would be subject to
export controls, but not to the restricted access and cumbersome
accounting rules that govern Type I equipment. The development of most
of the new equipment (both Type I and Type II) was to be carried out
through a 'Commercial Comsec Endorsement Program' in which industry

would commit the funds to develop equipment and the government would
mandate qualified products for government applications. Had this
program proceeded as originally envisioned, it would have supplanted
DES and returned tight control of U.S. cryptography to NSA.

Although the original vision called for far more Type II Comsec
equipment than Type I, ultimately, very little Type II equipment was
built. By the time the new products were ready for market, NSA had
changed its mind about their wide availability. The most visible
legacy of the NSDD-145 era is the STU-III telephone network in which
the vast majority of instruments are Type I and even those are fewer in
number than originally expected.

From a technical point of view, NSDD-145 made excellent sense. NSA
represented the greatest concentration of security expertise within the
government and was best positioned to oversee the development of new
families of products. The plan, however, failed to recognize the
realities of the contemporary world. American businesses and their
communications are inexorably intertwined with those of other
countries. In this environment, tamper resistant devices based on
secret algorithms are not a satisfactory basis for secure
communications.

Congress recognized the inappropriateness of NSDD-145 and in 1987,
passed the Computer Security Act. This act gave authority over
computer and communication security standards in the civilian world to
the organization that was shortly to be renamed the National Institute
of Standards and Technology. Regrettably, Congress failed to provide
adequate support for so large a task and NIST was unable to function
independently of NSA. Provisions of the act requiring NIST to consult
with NSA became the basis for a Memorandum of Understanding between the
two organizations that severely compromised NIST's independence. Under
the influence of the MOU, NIST appeared to be merely a front
organization for marketing NSA's products and three standards in
particular show that organization's dominance.

The 'Digital Signature Standard,' Federal Information Processing
Standard (or FIPS) 186 was designed at NSA and appears to have had the
objective of providing a digital signature system that could not be
readily applied to do encryption. To achieve this end, it competed
directly with RSA based digital signatures, which had become the
de-facto industry standard. Far from supplanting RSA, the DSS has
enjoyed only modest success, serving to decrease rather than increase
standardization.

FIPS 186 was accompanied by a separate standard for a technical
component of the signature process called a 'message digest algorithm.'
This, 'Secure Hash Standard' is FIPS 180. It too was developed at NSA
but, unlike its two companions, seems to enjoy substantial acceptance
in the commercial world.

It is worth noting that both FIPS 186 and FIPS 180 are based on
developments in the academic world. The Digital Signature Standard is
based on work done by Tahir ElGamal at Stanford University. The secure
hash algorithm is derived from the MD4 and MD5 algorithms designed
by Ron Rivest of MIT.

The most egregious example of NIST's lack of independence and the
ill effects of this lack of independence on the goals of the
Computer Security Act of 1987 is FIPS 186, the 'Escrowed Encryption
Standard.' FIPS 186 is unique among the Federal Information Processing
standards in not containing sufficient information to tell the reader
how to practice the standard. FIPS 186, specifies the use of a secret
cryptographic algorithm that is available to approved U.S.
organizations in the form of a tamper resistant chip, the infamous
'Clipper Chip.' The Clipper chip proved even less popular with its

proposed customer base than the Type II CCEP products that preceded
it. Not only were its workings secret, but it advertised an
unprecedented feature: all messages encrypted by Clipper chips could be
read by the U.S. government.

Perhaps the most remarkable thing about FIPS 186 is not that it is
based on a secret, but that the secret belongs to a department other
than the one that issued the standard. The secret 'Skipjack' algorithm
and other classified details of the Clipper chip are under the legal
and physical control of the Department of Defense and its contractors.
FIPS 186, however, was issued by a component of the Department of
Commerce. There can be no clearer evidence of NIST's allowing itself
to be controlled by NSA.

In order to understand the seriousness of these events for the
future of the United States, it suffices to look at the role
cryptography plays in today's world. We live in an era in which
electronic communication stands on a virtually equal footing with
face-to-face communication and written communication. Electronic
communication and the electronic commerce to which it is giving rise
are expected to revolutionize everything from entertainment to
education to medicine --- all over the world. The speed of
communication has accelerated a process of internationalization of
human society that began in the 19th Century with the railroad, the
telegraph and the steamship. Because security is an essential enabling
technology for these dreams, any security technology that expects to
support them must be available and trusted world-wide.

In addition to closer partnerships with other nations, we are
developing a more effective partnership between the government and
industry. It has come to be recognized that devices built exclusively
for government use, and even those built to government standards that
are not accepted industry standards, are far more expensive than
'Commercial, Off the Shelf' equipment. Government specific equipment
can also prove less satisfactory because larger markets provide a
financial base for product refinements that might not be possible in a
'government-only' market.

As an advisor to the public world on security technology, NSA
brings the advantage of great technical expertise. The advantage
of this expertise is overshadowed, however, by the fact that NSA also
brings to the table an important conflict of interest. It combines
within itself both the responsibility for protecting American
communications and the responsibility for spying on the communications
of other countries. The latter function, moreover, commands the vast
majority of NSA's budget and therefore dominates the formulation of
NSA's policies. The Agency is inclined to weigh the value of foreign
intelligence more heavily than the protection of the vast bulk of
American communications --- communications that are beyond its control
and whose protection is not likely to prove separable from improved
protection of information and communications throughout the world.

Under these circumstances, it is important for Congress to support
the development of independent centers of expertise in security,
both inside and outside the government. The defense of the nation is
of paramount importance and there can be no question that effective
collection of foreign intelligence is essential to that mission. On
the other hand, the nation's prosperity and its general well being are
just as important. These are the national characteristics the military
exists to defend.

In 1997, the National Institute of Standards and Technology has
begun to show a greater independence of thought and action in the
area of security that we have seen before. In January, the Federal
Register carried an announcement of the start of a project to develop a

successor to the twenty-year-old Data Encryption Standard (FIPS 46).
The announcement called for comments on criteria against which public
submissions of algorithms should be judged. The deadline for comments
was followed by a public meeting at which the comments were discussed.
This is a starting point far more appropriate to the development of a
public standard of such broad import than has been used previously. It
is therefore particularly gratifying to see that Congress is acting to
support NIST in its newly invigorated efforts to fulfill its role under
the Computer Security Act.

In its emphasis on open development of standards, recognition of
the importance of security products and developments from outside
our own borders, and on cooperation between the government and the
private sector, the Computer Security Enhancement Act of 1997 is a
strong step in the right direction. Improvement of the security of
communications and the growth of the many commercial opportunities
thereby created will be a source of both new jobs and new goods and
services for the American people.

Let me close by noting that there is one aspect of the Comments on
the Computer Security Enhancement Act of 1997 that I find
particularly gratifying. Early in my career in cryptography, I
predicted that, unlikely as it appeared at the time, there would be a
'normalization of relations' between the government and industry in the
field of cryptography. I noted that in the more familiar area of
physical security, the safes normally used by grocery stores to protect
money are stronger than those specifically designed to protect
classified documents.

In declaring that the Institute shall --- . . . (2) actively promote
the use of commercially available products to provide for the security
of sensitive information in Federal computer systems; the Act affirms my
belief that there will be a convergence between government and
commercial cryptographic practices --- a convergence that will lower
costs and improve security on both sides.

Whitfield Diffie, who holds the position of Distinguished Engineer
at Sun Microsystems, is best known for his 1975 discovery of the
concept of public key cryptography, for which he was awarded a
Doctorate in Technical Sciences (Honoris Causa) by the Swiss Federal
Institute of Technology in 1992.

For a dozen years prior to assuming his present position in 1991,
Diffie was Manager of Secure Systems Research for Northern Telecom,
functioning as the center of expertise in advanced security technologies
throughout the corporation. Among his achievements in this position was
the design of the key management architecture for NT's PDSO security system
for X.25 packet networks.

Diffie received a Bachelor of Science degree in mathematics
from the Massachusetts Institute of Technology in 1965. Prior to
becoming interested in cryptography, he worked on the development of
the Mathlab symbolic manipulation system --- sponsored jointly at
Mitre and the MIT Artificial Intelligence Laboratory --- and later on
proof of correctness of computer programs at Stanford University.

Since 1993, Diffie has worked largely in public policy, in the area of
cryptography. He has testified twice to the House and twice to the Senate.
His position --- in opposition to limitations on the business and personal
use of cryptography --- has been the subject of articles in the New York
Times Magazine, Wired, Omini, and Discover. The subject has also been
covered on the Discovery Channel, Equinox TV in Britain, and the Japanese
TV network NHK.

Notariety has provoked a number of awards, including:

   o IEEE Information Theory Society Best Paper Award for 1979.

   o IEEE Donald E. Fink award for 1981.

   o The 1994 Pioneer Award, given by The Electronic Frontiers
        Foundation for contribution to the quality of life in cyberspace.

   o The 1996 National Computer Systems Security Award given jointly by
        NIST and NSA.

   o The 1997 Louis E. Levy Medal from the Franklin Institute in
        Philadelphia.

   o The First ACM Paris Kanellakis Award for contribution to theory and
        practice in computer science.

Sun Microsystems, Inc.
Washington D.C. Public Policy Office
1300 I Street, N.W., Suite 420 East
Washington, D.C. 20005-3306
202 326 7520
202 326 7525 fax

June 19th, 1997

Mr. Richard Russell
Staff Director
Technology Subcommittee
Committee on Science
2319 Rayburn House Office Building
Washington, DC 20515

Dear Mr. Russell:

I understand that Dr. Diffie, a distinguished engineer at Sun Microsystems, will testify before your Committee today on the question of cryptography. I also understand that Congress requires witnesses to supply information regarding the extent to which their organizations rely on the federal government for funding to support research and development and other corporate activities.

Sun Microsystems will earn close to $9 Billion in revenue this year. The firm will earn roughly $800 Million from sales to the federal government. In addition, the firm has received a number of ATP technology grants. According to our technologists, the firm has not received any federal funds that support our efforts in cryptography. To the best of my knowledge, Sun Microsystems receives no other sources of federal funds.

Thank you for giving us an opportunity to testify before this Committee.

Sincerely,

Thomas Gann, Manager of
Federal Affairs and Head of the
Washington DC Office

CC: Donna Farmer, Counsel to the Committee

Mr. BRADY. Thank you, Dr. Diffie. And, I know, and each of the members knows, how difficult it is to try to summarize in 5 minutes. But, we do have your written statements.

And, we do have lots of questions afterwards. So, I appreciate it.

Mr. DIFFIE. I never feel it's any point in repeating the statement. You can read that. I tried to say something else.

Mr. BRADY. All of you are very patient. And, we appreciate it.

Mr. Walker.

STATEMENT OF STEPHEN T. WALKER, PRESIDENT AND CEO, TRUSTED INFORMATION SYSTEMS, INCORPORATED, GLENWOOD, MD

Mr. WALKER. Thank you. I appreciate the opportunity to be here this morning. And, I will try to be very brief.

My experience here today is, I think, relevant. I spent 20 years as a government employee starting with the National Security Agency and then the Defense Advanced Research Projects Agency back when the Arpanet was getting started, and the Office of the Secretary of Defense.

For the last 14 years, I have grown my company, Trusted Information Systems, from a one-man consulting shop to a 300 employee publicly traded company. But, perhaps more important than any of that, I had the opportunity to spend 5 years in the early 1990's as a member of the Computer Systems Security and Privacy Advisory Board.

When I was asked to be a member, I had really no clue what it was all about. There were times when the board really didn't quite know what it was supposed to be doing.

But, when the Clipper initiative and the digital signature standard and the other things came out in the early 1990's, the board served a very crucial role, for which I am glad you are recognizing the need of the board and that the efforts of the board need to be enhanced.

I strongly support both the 1987 Computer Security Act and the bill that you are considering here today. I strongly support the open discussion in the public of issues of computer security. In my 30 plus years of experience, I have observed on a number of occasions that when these discussions drift behind closed doors, things don't go well. I am a strong believer in the Advisory Board and have had considerable firsthand experience with its impact during some of its most effective periods.

As this bill points out, NIST has a very important role in directing assistance to the civilian agencies, a role which, for various reasons, as pointed out in Willis Ware's, the resolutions passed recently and his testimony, written testimony here, it hasn't done as well as it could have done. I think the provisions of this bill that strengthen the role of NIST in providing help to civilian agencies is very, very important.

I do worry—and will comment in a minute—on the provisions of the bill that assign NIST new product evaluation responsibilities. I'm not sure that my concern with that is the same as the Administration's concern; but, in fact, I believe that these are very difficult jobs that no one really knows very well how to do.

And, among other things, they will seriously distract NIST from the very important role that only it can do in providing help to the civilian agencies in understanding their computer security comments.

I would like to spend just a minute filling in a few niches of the history that Whit so eloquently commented on. The problems we are talking about here are not new. They date back, at least, to the introduction of DES back in the 1975 to 1977 time frame. Even then, there were struggles as to who should be providing advice to the civilian agencies on computer security and encryption.

In the late 1970's, President Carter signed Presidential Directive 24. Many people have forgotten about this one. It gave the National Telecommunications and Information Administration the responsibility for the unclassified use of encryption.

I know, from personal interactions with folks in the intelligence community, that caused great consternation and, in fact, was one of the things that prompted the passage of—or the signing by President Reagan of NSDD–145 in 1984 as a backlash to that directive. That one, as Whit has pointed out, gave the national security community and, in particular, the National Security Agency significant responsibilities in the civilian government area.

The Computer Security Act of 1987, of course, was a backlash, a counter-backlash, if you will, to the NSDD–145. And, it gave NIST the responsibility it has today, a very vital importance, to provide assistance to anyone handling sensitive and unclassified information, including the Department of Defense. And, that was always something that sort of stuck in various people's craws.

But, the debate, of course, didn't end there. The Memorandum of Understanding and the struggle over that, which Whit has commented on and I'm sure Marc will tell us something about a little bit later on—but I think the most important problem that followed the bill was the fact that the money wasn't there. Show me the money.

And, NIST did not have the ability to do the things that it was assigned to do in the bill. And, I'm glad that you all are considering improving that situation.

I note that at the height of the DOD's computer security activities in the late 1980's, they had a staff and resources 10 times the size of all of NIST's efforts in this area. I think Whit said pretty eloquently how that was going to work out.

The written statement of Willis Ware, which I have read and agree with, essentially said that the structure of the Act is satisfactory but that the implementation has had significant shortfalls. NIST has chosen in its use of its resources to focus more on research into new problems, next problems, than on the issue that is being pointed out here very strongly, that there are civil agencies who desperately need help solving some of these issues. And, they don't have the resources to figure out how to do that.

I think, as I said, this bill's focus on that is very important.

The Advisory Board is probably the most significant development in the Computer Security Act of 1987. The board has fostered open discussion and a public record of computer security issues such as the Clipper government key escrow system and the digital signature standard debates.

These would not have happened had there not been a board to lead the way in this and to help the government—help the public sector better understand the dangers of government key escrow. I strongly commend the efforts here to enhance the board.

The requirement that the Federal Information Processing Standards must come to the board for a recommendation before sending it to the Secretary of Commerce, I hope some reason prevails there because frequently the board has no information about some of those standards. But, had that provision been there, the escrowed encryption standard, which we talked about earlier, might have been handled differently. And, a very costly and failed effort might have been precluded earlier.

I'm glad to note that back in February, the Administration has decided to abandon government key escrow on the Fortezza card. And, so we've actually perhaps fixed this issue in a relatively short period of time in the normal evolution of government programs.

I am concerned about the portions of the bill that direct the NIST to perform evaluations and tests of information technology. In Section 4 of the bill, the new paragraph 6 is a very difficult task which, I will say, NIST is not well qualified to perform, but that's not to put NIST down. No one is well qualified to perform that job.

The Defense Department spent an enormous amount of time, some of which I was responsible for starting, trying to do that in the 1980's and early 1990's. And, they did not succeed at it. And, so I worry here that we may be launching them on a very expensive task which we are not going to be very happy with the results of.

Similarly, Section 7's tasking to evaluate the capabilities of foreign encryption, while representing a very highly desirable objective that we all would like to see the results of is, itself, also a very difficult task and one that no one in government or industry has been able to perform effectively at this point.

Both of these provisions are sending NIST off on a difficult, expensive and time consuming, I fear, wild goose chase, the result of which, I'm afraid, no one will be happy with. Please, review these provisions carefully while they will consume vast resources and seriously distract NIST from the vital role of providing that consistent and sensible advice to civilian agencies.

Finally, the last point I would like to make, while I am not fundamentally opposed to another NRC study on cryptography, I seriously wonder how much closer we will be to effective public key infrastructure after the study proposed here. Perhaps I will be pleasantly surprised.

I thank you very much for the opportunity to present my views and hope they are somewhat helpful to you.

[The prepared statement of Mr. Walker follows:]

Subcommittee on Technology
Committee on Science
U.S. House of Representatives
105th Congress, 1st Session

Hearing on the *Computer Security Enhancement Act of 1997*

June 19, 1997

Stephen T. Walker
President and CEO, Trusted Information Systems, Inc.
3060 Washington Road (Rt. 97)
Glenwood, MD 21738

Thank you very much for the opportunity to appear today and share my perspectives on enhancing computer security and on the role of the Computer System Security and Privacy Board (CSSPAB, or the Board). I am President and CEO of Trusted Information Systems, Inc. (TIS), which I founded in 1983. A publicly traded company, with offices in Maryland, Virginia, California and other U.S. locations, as well as in Europe, TIS specializes in research, product development, and consulting in the fields of computer and communications security.

My perspectives on computer security are based on over twenty years professional experience in system design and management within the Department of Defense and on my experience as an entrepreneur and businessman since founding TIS. My perspectives on the role and importance of the CSSPAB also reflect my participation as a Board member during 1990-95, a period which included the Board's 1993-94 deliberations on the U.S. government's "Clipper" escrowed encryption proposal.

My testimony today will highlight two of the ways in which the *Computer Security Enhancement Act of 1997* will benefit computer security in the civil agencies and elsewhere:

- by enhancing the computer system security capabilities of the National Institute of Standards and Technology (NIST) and moving practical assistance to federal agencies into the forefront of the NIST computer security mission; and
- by enhancing the role and resources of the Computer System Security and Privacy Board that was established by P.L. 100-235.

The remainder of my testimony will provide some historical and personal perspectives on the importance of openness and public visibility in the development and implementation of federal computer security standards and, therefore, why it is so important to preserve and enhance the functions of the Computer System Security and Privacy Board.

I strongly support the provisions of the Act that will accomplish the objectives of strengthening NIST's mission and capabilities for providing computer system security guidance and assistance to federal agencies. I also strongly support the provisions of the Act that will enhance the role and resources of the Computer System Security and Privacy Board.

However, experience has shown that security product testing and evaluation, particularly qualitative testing and evaluation, is difficult, contentious, and expensive. As we have seen in other government product evaluation programs, it is very hard to establish good criteria, perform evaluations, and defend results. Therefore, I believe it would make far better use of NIST's resources and capabilities to have them concentrate on doing the best job possible in helping federal agencies to protect their computer systems and in coordinating federal emergency response efforts, rather than requiring NIST to also perform various types of product testing and evaluation (e.g., to determine suitability for use by federal agencies, or to determine capabilities of foreign products). Therefore, I have reservations about the sections of the Act that would require NIST to do product testing and evaluation.

<u>Enhanced NIST Capabilities</u>

The *Computer Security Enhancement Act* would enhance the capabilities of the National Institute of Standards and Technology (NIST) for providing computer system security guidance and assistance to federal agencies. I strongly support the language in Section 4 of the Act that would explicitly charter NIST with helping federal agencies to protect their networks, as well as with coordinating federal response efforts when those networks are attacked.

These are areas that have long needed strengthening. NIST's current mandate does not place adequate priority on direct provision of practical, *system-level* security assistance and guidance to the civil agencies as they seek to select and deploy security solutions in a timely and cost-effective manner, as required by the revised Appendix III of OMB Circular A-130.

In this regard, it is also important to note that Section 5 of the Act requires NIST to emphasize the development of *technology-neutral* policy guidelines for federal agency computer security practices, as well as to promote use of commercially available security products by the agencies. Thus, the Act recognizes that it is no longer necessary or appropriate to develop "government-only" technologies or standards for use in safeguarding non-classified information. Industry-led, market driven security solutions are available that can (and do) meet the needs of both government and private-sector customers.

Toward these ends, it might be useful to include explanatory language in the report accompanying the *Computer Security Enhancement Act* that would provide additional guidance as to:

- NIST participation in "implementations of encryption technologies in order to develop required standards and guidelines," in terms of the types of activities, pilot projects, etc. that would be envisioned by Section 5 of the Act; and
- mechanisms by which the private sector would request assistance from NIST in establishing voluntary standards, as envisioned by Section 3 of the Act.

<u>Enhanced Board Capabilities</u>

The principal focus of my testimony today regarding the *Computer Security Enhancement Act of 1997* is on the important role the Computer System Security and Privacy Board has played, and should continue to play, in the development and implementation of computer security guidance for the civil agencies.

The increased financial resources for FY98 and FY99 and the enhanced Board authorities for issue identification, public meetings, report preparation, and publication provided by Section 6 of the *Computer Security Enhancement Act* will enable the Board to address important issues related to computer security, privacy, and cryptography in a more proactive and extensive fashion that has been possible with relatively limited resources to date.

Moreover, providing a mechanism in Section 6 through which Board input can be taken into account by the Secretary of Commerce prior to the promulgation of certain computer security standards and guidelines can be beneficial in providing additional opportunity for openness and public participation in their development. Based on my experiences, I believe that this mechanism would have been both appropriate and useful during the promulgation of the Digital Signature Standard and the Escrowed Encryption Standard. However, it need not be the case that the Board will wish to (or be able to) provide recommendations for each and every computer security standard or guideline, so some discretion on the part of the Board in this regard would also be desirable.

<u>Necessity of Preserving and Strengthening the CSSPAB</u>

Compared to 1987, given today's technical, economic, and political environment, I believe there is even greater need for open processes in developing and implementing federal information security policies and standards. I think it would be hard for anyone to make an argument for "less openness" in terms of process.

The CSSPAB has consistently played a vital role in <u>creating</u> and preserving open channels for public visibility and public input into the processes by which this nation's cryptography policies have developed during the decade. For example, in 1992, prompted by controversies over the then-proposed Digital Signature Standard, the Board unanimously approved a resolution that "a national level review of the positive and negative implications of the widespread use of public and secret key cryptography" was required in order to produce a "national policy concerning the use of cryptography in unclassified/sensitive government and the private sector."[1]

A year later, after the "surprise" April 1993 introduction of the escrowed-encryption initiative and at the request of the NIST Deputy Director, the Board devoted its June 1993 meeting to hearing public views on what was then called "Clipper." The Board thereafter unanimously resolved to gather additional public and government input and recommended that the Administration's ongoing cryptography policy review take note of the "serious concerns and problems" that the CSSPAB had identified.[2] The Board subsequently held four more days of public hearings, confirmed there were serious concerns to be resolved, and strengthened its views on the importance of a broad national cryptography policy review, including Congress, in order to resolve how the interests of law enforcement, national security, U.S. industry, and individual persons might best be protected.[3]

These actions by the Board provided an open forum in which government views, as well as public views, could be heard. The Board created a public record for study of national cryptography policy.[4] Perhaps most importantly, the Board assembled the only public record of ongoing government activities and progress in the escrowed-encryption initiative.

Absent that open forum and public record, today the "encryption dilemma" would probably be even more confusing than it is. But there _was_ an open forum and a public record, because there _was_ a Computer System Security and Privacy Board, established by the Computer Security Act of 1987.

The nation still needs that Board in place, and a strengthened Board at that, its role and resources enhanced commensurate with the increased importance of computer systems and networks in business, government, and everyday life.

Thank you for the opportunity to present my views. If additional information or discussions would be helpful to the Subcommittee, your colleagues, or your staffs, please let me know how I can be of assistance as you move forward with this bill.

---

[1]   CSSPAB Resolution No. 1, Mar. 18, 1992.

[2]   CSSPAB Resolution No. 1, June 4, 1993.

[3]   CSSPAB Resolutions 93-5 and 93-6 of September 1-2, 1993.

[4]   In 1993, the CSSPAB endorsed the National Research Council study that resulted in the 1996 _CRISIS_ report as the study that "best accomplishes" the Board's repeated calls for a national cryptography study. CSSPAB Resolution 93-7, December 8-9, 1993.

Biographical and Background Information

Stephen T. Walker is the President, and Chief Executive Officer of Trusted Information Systems, Inc., which he founded in 1983 and today employs approximately 300 personnel. His background includes twenty-two years as an employee of the Department of Defense at the National Security Agency, the Advanced Research Projects Agency, and the Office of the Secretary of Defense. Mr. Walker has over 35 years of experience in system design and program management. He is nationally recognized for his pioneering work on the DoD Computer Security Initiative, establishment of the National Computer Security Center and the Defense Data Network, and extensive experience with the design and implementation of large-scale computer networks and information systems. In 1984, Mr. Walker received the Secretary of Defense Meritorious Civilian Service Award, and in October 1988, he received the first National Computer System Security Award. In March 1995, Mr. Walker was the recipient of Federal Computer Week's Federal 100 Award. He served as a member of the Congressionally chartered Computer System Security and Privacy Advisory Board, which was established as part of the Computer Security Act of 1987. On several occasions, he has testified before the U.S. Congress as an expert on computer and communications security.

Trusted Information Systems, Inc., (TIS), has been dedicated to providing computer and communications security solutions for business information systems for over a decade. Through a combination of advanced research and engineering, system security analysis, practical and affordable solutions, and training, TIS is transforming the Internet into a safe place to do business. TIS is a leading provider of comprehensive security solutions for protection of computer networks, including global Internet-based systems, internal networks and individual workstations and laptops. The company develops, markets, licenses and supports the Gauntlet® family of firewall products and other network security products, and provides cryptography and security consulting training, advanced research and engineering, and services for commercial and government customers. TIS is a publicly traded company (Nasdaq: TISX); the TIS home page on the World Wide Web is http://www.tis.com.

STEPHEN T. WALKER
President and CEO
Trusted Information Systems, Inc.

Mr. Walker has over 35 years of experience in system design and program management. He is nationally recognized for his pioneering work on the DoD Computer Security Initiative, establishment of the National Computer Security Center and the Defense Data Network, and extensive experience with the design and implementation of large-scale computer networks and information systems. In 1984, Mr. Walker received the Secretary of Defense Meritorious Civilian Service Award, and in October 1988, he received the first National Computer System Security Award. In March 1995, Mr. Walker was the recipient of Federal Computer Week's Federal 100 Award. From 1990 to 1995, he served as a member of the Congressionally chartered Computer System Security and Privacy Advisory Board, which was established as part of the Computer Security Act of 1987. On several occasions, he has testified before the U.S. Congress as an expert on computer and communications security.

EXPERIENCE

1983 - Present:

Trusted Information Systems, Inc. (TIS), Glenwood, MD

Stephen T. Walker is the President and Chief Executive Officer of Trusted Information Systems, Inc. (Nasdaq: TISX), which he founded in 1983. TIS currently employs approximately 300 personnel. Through a combination of advanced research and engineering, system security analysis, development of practical and affordable security solutions, and training, TIS has become a leading provider of comprehensive security solutions for protection of computer networks, including global Internet-based systems, internal networks and individual workstations and laptops. TIS develops, markets, licenses, and supports the Gauntlet family of firewall products and other network security products, and provides cryptography and security consulting training, advanced research and engineering, and services for commercial and government customers.

1980 - 1983:

Office of the Secretary of Defense, Pentagon, Director of Information Systems, for the Undersecretary for Research and Engineering, Washington, DC

Senior technical advisor for the Secretary of Defense for the World Wide Military Command and Control System (WWMCCS) Information System (WIS) and the Defense Communications System. Including Defense Data and Switching Networks; initiated major restructuring of DOD data communications architecture. Principal advocate for termination of Autodin II and establishment of DDN. Founded DoD Computer Security Evaluation Center. Conducted highly successful seminars on DoD Computer Security Initiative, and chaired Network System Security Subcommittee of National COMSEC Committee. Executive Secretary, Defense Science Board Task Force on Autodin II. Received SECDEF Meritorious Civilian Service Medal.

STEPHEN T. WALKER
PAGE 2

1978 - 1980:

Office of the Secretary of Defense, Pentagon, Washington D.C., Assist. Secretary of Defense for Communications, Command, Control and Intelligence, ASD (C3I), Information Systems Directorate, ASD (C3I)

Established DoD Computer Security Initiative; fostered computer industry development of trusted ADP systems; coordinated all DoD R&D in computer security; developed trusted ADP evaluation and accreditation procedures; established DoD data network protocol standardization program. Member, Critical Technology Export Group, DNA Computer Advisory Board; frequent speaker at technical conferences; chairman of sessions at NCC 1979, 1980. **1974 - 1978:**

Defense Advanced Research Projects Agency, Arlington, VA, Program Manager, Information Processing Techniques Office

Managed advanced research projects in system and network security, message technology, intelligent terminals, and DBMS. Initiated development of several trusted computer systems, CINCPAC Military Message Experiment, network security activities. Managed ARPAnet, including transfer to operational status.

1966 - 1974:

National Security Agency, Fort Meade, MD Research & Development Organization, Computer Sciences Division

Principal investigator of NSA's computer networking architecture. Recommended ARPAnet technology adopted and still in use. Project leader for R&D in computer networking, interactive graphic displays, and high order languages. Programming experience on wide range of computer systems.

EDUCATION

MS, Electrical Engineering, University of Maryland, 1968
BS, Electrical Engineering, Northeastern University, 1966

06/97

TRUSTED INFORMATION SYSTEMS DISCLOSURE STATEMENT FOR HEARING

AGENCY	CONTRACT #	SUBCONTRACT	VALUE
Booz-Allen Hamilton	MDA904-96-C-1553	Subc #14317DS100	$determined by task orders
Booz-Allen Hamilton	MDA904-96-C-1651	Subc #14066DS103	$ 639,964
NCCOSC	XXXXXX-93-D-1824		$1,124,198
SAIC	N66001-96-D-8607	Subc#4500086923	$115,003
SAIC	DASG60-96-C-0064	Subc ~L4500097252	$119, 163
Teknowledge	Unknown	Letter authorization	$307, 108
Boeing Co./Defense & Space Group	F30602-96-C-0318	Purchase Contract No. JG8988	$224,758
Boeing Company	Unknown	Purchase Contract No. JM1802	$ 59,224
Ft. Huachuca, *AZ*	DABT63-95-C-0044		$305,453
Rome Labs, New York	F30602-96-C-0333		$1,375,598
Maryland Procurement	MDA904-95-P-5050		$25,000
Maryland Procurement	MDA904-96-P-9394		$10,000
CSC	MDA904-93-C-B053		$314,768
DMSO	XXXXXX-93-D-1824		$384,559
EIT	Subc ~Eit-001		$691,3 84
Eagan, McAllister	PO #96C-0617		$42,375
Ft. Huachuca, *AZ*	DABT63-95-C-0018		$2,839,687
Ft. Huachuca, AZ	DABT63-92-C-0020		$2,465,914
Hughes Aircraft	P 0 ~JRI28376SFI/Rev Ltr		$260,000
L & E Associates	PO #0157		$119,701
L & E Associates	PO #0110		$78,216
Maryland Procurement	MDA904-95-C-4097		$183,701
Maryland Procurement	MDA904-96-C-0535		$476,477
Rome Laboratories	F30602-95-C-0290		$2,356,797

Mr. BRADY. You bet. Thank you, Mr. Walker. Mr. Bidzos, I understand you've had a big week. So, I look forward to your remarks.

STATEMENT OF D. JAMES BIDZOS, PRESIDENT, RSA DATA SECURITY, INCORPORATED, REDWOOD CITY, CA

Mr. BIDZOS. Thank you, Mr. Chairman. I also want to thank the Committee for the opportunity to be here.

I will make a few remarks, try to keep them brief. And, of course, I've submitted a statement.

Let me just say right up front that I'm very supportive of H.R. 1903. I think it is timely, important and offers the potential for the best return on investment in legislation that I've seen in the 12 years, half the time of some of these other gentlemen, that I've been in the business.

But, before I start, I hope I can steal 45 seconds to respond to what we've heard about Section 7 of the bill. I think the Committee has shown a little more wisdom than it is getting credit for. And, let me suggest both to Mr. Bachula and also to my friend, Steve, why I think that might be very, very appropriate.

The fastest growing software company in Germany is a company called Braukat. Braukat's business consists exclusively of replacing the encryption in American-made products that are sold in Germany.

So, when Netscape and Microsoft ship a product to Germany, to a German customer, with the weakened encryption that's required by our export regulations, Braukat comes in and replaces it with a strong encryption similar to, this is all encryption that my company designed, similar to the encryption that is in the U.S. version.

So, first of all, if it isn't the Commerce Department's responsibility to protect U.S. industry by identifying and monitoring this type of activity, whose job is it? I think the bill is right on the money in tasking NIST with those kinds of responsibilities.

I think the Commerce Department, as I will talk about in a moment, in the area of encryption has really let industry down in many, many ways. This is an excellent opportunity to get it back.

It is not difficult. It is not a distraction. It's not technically difficult to determine simply and solely if a foreign company has been able to successfully replace cryptography.

And, I am absolutely confident that should NIST ask them that Netscape and Microsoft would be delighted to make technical resources available if there is even the slimmest hope of some policy change that could be effected by their efforts. So, I think it is neither difficult nor inappropriate for NIST to take on this role.

It is perfectly appropriate for the Commerce Department to be helping U.S. industry in this way.

First of all, let me just say a few words about myself and my company. My company is RSA Data Security. It has been around since 1982. I've been running it for a little over 11 years.

We've been fortunate in that we've designed some very useful technology that has found great commercial success. Our encryption technology is embedded in just about every product that I suspect everybody in this room uses.

If you've surfed the net with Netscape Navigator, Microsoft Internet Explorer, if you use Lotus notes, if you use products from Oracle, IBM, AT&T, right on down the line, 400 companies, 100 million copies of products that contain our encryption technology, then you are an encryption user. The next time you are using Netscape Navigator, go to the About Netscape and go to the bit about security, and you will find an incredible tutorial about encryption that will tell you a lot about what this technology is doing.

Now, as unbelievable as what I am about to say may sound, in spite of the fact that these 100 million copies of off-the-shelf products exist and are being used by U.S. industry to reinvest themselves, to make themselves more efficient, to do all the things we read about all the time, companies and industries getting turned upside down by the World Wide Web, it is the policy of this Administration that those products cannot be used by civilian agencies of the Federal Government. They are required to use the products based on standard that Dr. Diffie described, the escrowed encryption standard, not what one might call one of the great successes of NIST in the area of standardization or NSA in its short foray into commercial product marketing and development; and, the digital signature standard which, as Dr. Diffie said, was an attempt to displace an existing standard—always a hard thing to do at best, not very successful.

The unfortunate victims of this policy are the civilian agencies of the Federal Government, who are simply trying to provide more security, which the Act directed them to do in 1987. It was a very timely and very good Act.

And, they are finding it very difficult to do that. They either have to pay a huge amount of money for products that contain technology that nobody really wants to support, which are the existing federal standards; or, they have to go through a very complex and difficult waiver process, although the Environmental Protection Agency and the Department of Agriculture have both done that; or, they have to do nothing at all and leave these systems vulnerable. And, obviously, that's unacceptable.

This Committee has recognized that. And, that is one of the very important things that this Act can fix.

The Computer Security Act was an example of great timing and good leadership in 1987. Obviously, the Congress identified the need for computer security.

It gave NIST the responsibility to provide the leadership in computer security for the federal agencies of government. Unfortunately, for reasons that we don't have time to discuss here, NIST was unable to take advantage of the opportunity created for it by Congress.

Perhaps it was the MOU. Perhaps it was a lot of other things.

NIST has done many good things in the area of computer security. But, when it comes to encryption, I'm afraid that they have turned the relationship with industry into an adversarial relationship when, in fact, there was a tremendous opportunity to work with industry; that while it has been missed, we have an opportunity now to correct it. And, I think that's what H.R. 1903 does.

I mentioned how unbelievable it is that in this day and age with that sort of distribution of 100 million products that can be used to reinvent government, according to the Vice President's own initiative, 40 of the 45 pilots in the Vice President's initiative, by the way, use the "illegal technology." This bill would fix all of that.

This bill would direct NIST to get together with industry, to adopt market solutions, give NIST an opportunity to restore its leadership and its credibility with U.S. industry, which would provide an excellent benefit, an excellent result, which is giving the civilian federal agencies, all 120 some of them, the opportunity to simply address the computer security need that they understand and that is so important to them right now.

So, the bill would do wonderful things. It would cause NIST to adopt market solutions. It would give them the opportunity to follow up on these three initiatives that were discussed—the advanced encryption standard which, in light of today's story in the "Wall Street Journal," if you saw it, it's critically important. The 25 year old DES was broken for the first time in history.

A momentous event happened within hours of the appearance of the McCain/Kerrey bill. No time to get into that today either.

But, at any rate, this demonstrates how important it is for NIST to take initiative. It's unfortunate that within 48 hours after DES was broken we are talking about an advanced encryption standard process that will probably take a couple of years.

Wouldn't it have been very, very good and so much better for us if this process had been started 2 or 3 years ago? We would be ahead of the curve instead of behind it.

The other thing that NIST could do is finish its correction of its signature standard and recognize what has gone on in industry.

And, the third thing it could do is complete its key management FIPS effort which, by the way, FOYI documents found by Epic show that NIST discovered, identified and recognized the need for a key management standard in 1989. And, we still don't have one today. This bill would allow them to get moving on it.

So, basically, in summary, the overall return on investment for this legislation is incredibly high. I think this is a classic example of a great return on a small piece of legislation that will pay dividends throughout the Federal Government, provide enhanced computer security.

It's just hard to see any down side whatsoever to this. And, I made my comments about Section 7. I won't say anymore.

So, basically, the benefits would be the additional security of federal systems, the restoring of NIST's opportunity to take a leadership role and partner with industry, benefit from all of that technology, bring it to federal agencies, be a showcase for computer security solutions, and lead rather than fight over waivers and other things with these federal agencies.

So, I strongly support this legislation. I want to thank the Committee and Madam Chairwoman for their leadership, for the willingness to pursue this and to invest the time.

It's timely. It's important. I couldn't be happier about it.

Thank you very much.

[The prepared statement of Mr. Bidzos follows:]

TESTIMONY OF

D. JAMES BIDZOS, PRESIDENT

RSA DATA SECURITY, INC.

HTTP://WWW.RSA.COM

ON

THE COMPUTER SECURITY ENHANCEMENT ACT OF 1997

BEFORE THE
HOUSE COMMITTEE ON SCIENCE
SUBCOMMITTEE ON TECHNOLOGY

JUNE 19, 1997

My name is D. James Bidzos. I am the President of RSA Data Security, Inc., which is located in Redwood City, California. My company is the world's leading provider of commercial encryption products. Our technology is found in the most popular hardware and software products developed by such leading companies as Netscape Communications, IBM, Lotus, Microsoft, Oracle and hundred of other vendors. RSA encryption is an integral part of an estimated ninety million copies of various commercial hardware and software applications.

RSA Data Security hosts an annual cryptography conference. This has become a major national forum for the discussion of cryptography policy issues and the latest advances in commercial encryption technology. The 1997 conference, held in January, attracted more that three thousand participants. RSA Data Security has also established an office in Tokyo, Japan, where we have found considerable interest in the use of cryptography for electronic commerce applications. We were also instrumental in the founding of an independent company, VeriSign, Inc. This company provides digital identification and authentication services for individuals and companies wishing to engage in secure electronic commerce activities.

My company, along with the over four hundred other companies who have licensed RSA cryptographic products, together with VeriSign provided digital identities, comprise an emerging national public key infrastructure. This nascent infrastructure is poised to meet the needs of the American public and private sectors for secure electronic commerce and government services.

I. THE IMPORTANCE OF THE COMPUTER SECURITY ACT OF 1987.

The passage of the Computer Security Act of 1987 was an important landmark in the evolution of the government's attempts to deal with the security issues resulting from the extensive use of computer technology by federal agencies. The Congress correctly recognized that many agencies of the government were not properly addressing their computer security problems, with the result that federal programs and activities were vulnerable to service disruptions, criminal activities, and the compromise of sensitive personal information.

Another major issue that the Congress confronted in 1987 was the question of leadership within the federal government on computer security matters. The Congress was confronted with an environment where a component of the Defense Department, the National Security Agency (NSA), had been placed in control of computer security policy for the entire government, to include civil agencies such as the Social Security Administration and the Department of Education.

Many individuals, especially those in the academic, banking, information, and computer communities, viewed NSA as the wrong agency for exercising these leadership responsibilities for systems security across the entire federal government. These concerns were also echoed by segments of the business community who reacted negatively to the attempt to expand the definition of "sensitive but unclassified information" to include national security concerns. This was viewed as having a potentially negative impact on public access to unclassified information.

With the passage of the Computer Security Act (PL 100-235), the Congress, correctly in my view, reversed the leadership model created during the Reagan administration and mandated that the National Institute of Standards and Technology (NIST), then known as the National Bureau of Standards provide leadership to the unclassified systems community within the government. Congress viewed the NIST standards program as the vehicle through which this leadership would be exercised. The Congress recognized that a civil agency, NIST, should provide leadership to the unclassified federal community is a fundamental principle that the Computer Security Enhancement Act of 1997 preserves and seeks to enhance. I fully endorse and support this continuing basic separation of responsibilities and authorities between NIST and NSA.

However, the passage of the Computer Security Act of 1987 failed to achieve some of the expectations of the sponsors of the original act. This shortfall occurred primarily in the field of cryptography. I believe that NIST did not sufficiently leverage its authority and ability to fully involve the energy and productivity of the US computer and communications industry for the benefit of the civil agencies of the government, and ultimately the citizens/taxpayers of this country.

The Digital Signature and Escrowed Encryption standards are prime examples of unsuccessful cryptography initiatives that have hampered the ability of government agencies to deliver secure electronic services. The lack of market acceptance of these technologies has resulted in an environment where the federal government effectively cut itself off from the advances being made in commercial cryptographic products. Only within the past few weeks have the necessary steps been initiated to allow federal agencies to take full advantage of the market driven, cost effective cryptographic solutions being delivered by US hardware and software product vendors.

II. NIST'S RELATIONSHIP WITH THE PRIVATE SECTOR

NIST, and its predecessor organization, has a long and distinguished history of working effectively with, and in support of the private sector on a variety of computer security matters. In the field of cryptography, the development of the Data Encryption Standard (DES) is the classic example of productive collaboration between NIST and the private sector. However since the passage of PL 100-235, NIST has consistently disappointed the private sector, and many of its government customers, with its activities in the field of cryptography.

The recent attempts by NIST to implement non-market driven cryptographic standards underscore that the time has past where the government can influence the private sector's use of cryptography by manipulating the standards process. These unsuccessful forays, which have been undertake to shape the market, have only served to weakened NIST's creditability in the field of cryptography.

This proposed law correctly seeks to restore NIST's technical leadership by enhancing its ability to act independently in this increasingly important segment of information technology. We in industry need a strong, independent NIST that is able to clearly articulate the needs of their government customers for encryption based confidentiality and authentication products. The civil agencies also need a viable center of cryptographic excellence at NIST to assist the unclassified systems community with the challenges they face in maximizing the benefits of effectively using commercial off-the-shelf encryption products.

The Computer Security Enhancement Act of 1997 correctly stipulates that NIST will place primary reliance in the development of cryptographic standards upon the technology "...driven by market forces rather than by Government imposed requirements". This is a exactly the statutory direction that should be established to help NIST focus its computer security program on assisting its primary customers, the agencies that operate unclassified information systems.

Within the past several months NIST has made three important announcements which deserve positive recognition. These indicate a recognition on the part of NIST to accommodate market driven cryptography standards within the federal environment. The first of these was the announcement of their intent to start the process leading to the adoption of an Advanced Encryption Standard. The open process which NIST has adopted to select a replacement algorithm is the type of public-private sector partnership that should characterize the NIST cryptography program. This initiative is consistent with the spirit and intent of this proposed legislation.

I would also like to express my support for the recent move that NIST made to modify the existing Federal Digital Signature Standard to include the RSA algorithm. This will start the process of correcting the mistake that NIST made in 1993 in selecting a NSA developed algorithm as the basis for this standard. The Federal agency user community has been the loser as a result of this decision, as they have been denied access to the commercial products needed to realize the Administration's goals of creating an electronic government. I would also like to note that of the forty-five digital signature demonstrations projects sponsored by the Government Information Technology Services Board, approximately forty will use the RSA cryptography found in a variety of commercial products.

The third initiative recently announced by NIST, is the development of a cryptographic key management standard, based upon multiple public key algorithms. Such a standard has long been needed by the federal user community and is an integral component of any comprehensive network security solution. NIST recognized the requirement for such a standard in 1989, according to a NIST and NSA documents obtained over the past few years through the Freedom of Information Act process.

III. Impact of the Computer Security Enhancement Act of 1997.

The passage of this legislation will have a positive impact upon the security of federal information systems. This will result from the redirection of NIST's efforts in the field of computer security from long term research to working directly with federal agencies to resolve the security issues they are facing in operational information systems using existing commercial technology. The emphasis upon the issue of " unauthorized access" will also help NIST to concentrate on one of the more important issues that confronts the users of both public and private sector information systems. Improvements in this one aspect of the computer security problem can produce a great return on investment.

In a more fundamental sense this law recognizes that the products that federal agencies are going to employ for protecting government information systems will be designed and built in response to market driven requirements. The most significant premise of this proposed legislation is that it recognizes the dynamic nature of the market place and seeks to assure that government unclassified systems are secured through the use of commercial technology that adheres to widely accepted standards.

In conclusion, this very important legislation will allow the non-classified agencies of the US government to take advantage of the infrastructure which industry has built over the last ten years. For example, the Social Security Administration could have purchased a single server to issue a digital credential, called a certificate, and issued these certificates to its clients, the citizens of this nation. Anyone with Internet access could then make use of these certificates because every version of very web browser made by Netscape and Microsoft, over 80 million copies, are "crypto and certificate enabled". This same technology is that VISA and MasterCard are employing to support the use of electronic credit card purchases on the Internet.

This emerging infrastructure could be utilized by any agency, such as the IRS, SSA, or the Department of Education needing secure and authenticated communications between the agency and taxpayers and citizens. A strong and vigorous NIST, clear in its mission, and determined to support the work of the civil agencies can be an essential catalyst in realizing the full power of public key cryptography for the benefit of the citizens of this country.

I fully support the spirit and intent of this legislation.

IV. Comments on Specific Provisions of the Computer Security Enhancement Act of 1997. I have some specific comments on the provisions of the bill, and these are covered in my formal statement.

--Section 2 (a) (5). Foreign Availability. This is a very important component of this statute. Foreign availability must be an significant component of any export control regime for commercial encryption products. The Administration's interim s export control restrictions, issued at the end of 1996, specifically exclude foreign availability as a consideration in granting export approvals for commercial cryptography products. Without foreign availability being a mandatory consideration, export control determinations will be made in an environment that is detached from the reality of the global market place.

—Sec 3. Public Key Management Standards. I am somewhat neutral on this provision as I am concerned that it could be exploited to push government developed standard for key recovery into the private sector before any fundamental public policy decisions have been made on the desirability, feasibility and legality of integrating key recovery into the national and global information infrastructure. If NIST were recognized as an honest broker, could it have a significant role to play in the development of needed standards the public key infrastructure? The answer to this is Yes, but I would like to bring to the committee's attention the fact that a public key infrastructure is beginning to emerge independent of any leadership role played by NIST. The private sector users and product suppliers are creating the fundamental components of this infrastructure through the forces of the market.

--Sec 4. Security of Federal Computers and Networks. The underlying emphasis of this section of the bill on stimulating the use of the security features designed into commercial products is one of the more important aspects of this proposed piece of legislation. I believe that if the government is to receive full value for the money spent on information technology, federal agencies should be free and, indeed encouraged, to use the security functionality that is integrated into the popular commercial products found in the market place. NIST can fulfill a very useful function by providing the technical leadership needed by federal agencies in maximizing their investment in commercial hardware and software computer and communication products. Correspondingly, if the government is going to rely on commercial products, agencies need to understand if security flaws or vulnerabilities exist in a given product. In this respect NIST is uniquely positioned to use its own internal resources, as well as those of its National Voluntary Laboratory program to undertake this responsibility.

--Sec 5. Computer Security Implementation. I am somewhat uncertain on the intent of the part three of this section. It would appear to be virtually impossible for NIST to participate in the design and implementation of cryptographic technology in commercial products. Most companies would be unwilling to permit the involvement of government employees in decisions that affect the design of commercial products. In this respect the FIPS 140-1 validation program operated by NIST can be a valuable resource for obtaining some of the information specified in this section.

—Section 6. Enhancing the Role of the Computer Systems Security and Privacy Advisory Board. I strongly support the provisions of this section which seek to enhance the stature and capabilities of the Advisory Board. This group has been an underutilized resource throughout its existence. Many dedicated and knowledgeable security professionals and government managers have served on this board. In the field of cryptography policy the Board has performed a highly useful public service. It issued the call for a review of national cryptographic policy, expressed concern about the adoption of a digital signature standard that was not supported by the commercial market, and created an important public record during its public forum on the Clipper Chip proposal. This legislation correctly seeks to enhance the ability of the Computer Systems Security and Privacy Advisory Board to provide insights for the Executive and Legislative branches on emerging issues affecting the security of federal information systems.

-6-

I would also like to suggest that the Advisory Board be encouraged to hold meetings outside of the Washington area. I'm sure that the Board could gain additional needed perspectives by holding public meetings in other parts of the country.

--Section 7. International Assessment of Encryption Technologies. I believe that this is a worthwhile activity, as it is important that this work be undertaken in an open environment. In the past few years the Software Publishers Association and Trusted Information Systems have contributed some very useful data to the cryptography debate by collecting information on foreign cryptography products and making this available in an unclassified manner to interested parties.

--Section 9 (2). Miscellaneous Amendments. It appears that one of the impacts of this aspect of the proposed law will be the requirement to revise the 1989 NIST/NSA Memorandum of Understanding.

--Section 12. Study of Public Key Infrastructure. This has the potential of being a very useful activity; however, developments in the use of public key are proceeding at such a pace that an eighteen month study may not produce the timely insights desired by the Congress

RSA Data Security.
A Security Dynamics Company

100 Marine Pk

Suite 500

Redwood City

California, 94

415/595-878

415/595-157

http://www.rsa

Biography: D. James Bidzos, President and CEO, RSA Data Security, Inc.

Jim Bidzos has been President of RSA Data Security for over eleven years. Under his leadership, RSA has become the worldwide de facto standard for encryption, being included in such products as Netscape Navigator, Lotus Notes, Novell Netware, Intuit's Quicken, and Microsoft Windows 95. there are over 100 million copies of RSA's software in use today. No other company in the world comes close to matching this successful development of encryption technology. In fact, virtually the entire debate over the export of encryption revolves around the RSA technology.

Recognized as a visionary and pioneer in the computer industry, Mr. Bidzos is credited with tirelessly promoting the need for encryption since the mid-1980's. If you use products from IBM, ATT, Lotus, Sun, DEC, Novell, Netscape, Spyglass, or over three hundred others, you are already using RSA. Soon, you'll be using RSA to do credit card transactions on the net. VISA, MasterCard, IBM, Microsoft, Netscape, CyberCash, and Digicash, among others all use RSA in their electronic money products and services.

On July 29, 1996, Security Dynamics and RSA announced the completion of a merger. In connection with the merger, Security Dynamics Board of Directors elected Mr. Bidzos as a director and an executive vice president of the company. (Mr. Bidzos continues to hold the post of Chief Executive of RSA.) The marriage of RSA and Security Dynamics positioned the new combined Company as the undisputed leader of the security industry. The revenue of the combined companies is projected to be in excess of $100 million in 1997.

In 1994, Mr. Bidzos was involved as an investor in the founding of both Netscape and Cybercash, two leading Internet software companies. In early 1995, Mr. Bidzos personally founded VeriSign, a company that is the world leader in its field. VeriSign provides products and services that allow for the identification of parties on the other end of an electronic transaction or session on the Internet. He brought VISA, Ameritech, Mitsubishi, and others in as founding investors. Verisign's investors today include Microsoft, Cisco, Reuters, Merrill Lynch, Gemplus, and others. Mr. Bidzos serves as Chairman of the Board of VeriSign. Mr. Bidzos also serves on the board of directors of both RSA and VeriSign subsidiaries in Japan. In 1996, Mr. Bidzos founded Nihon RSA, a Tokyo-based subsidiary of RSA Data Security. Its investors include NTT, Sony, Sharp, NEC, Sanwa Bank, Sumitomo Bank, and others. Nihon RSA is Japan's premier encryption company.

With RSA Data Security, Verisign, and Nihon RSA, Mr. Bidzos has built a worldwide public key infrastructure. The security provided by RSA has revolutionized the Internet; yet RSA's success has been achieved in spite of intense opposition from the National Security Agency. NSA has, through government standards-making authority, export controls, and purchasing power, attempted to stop the spread of RSA technology. Even today, in 1997, standards controlled by NSA do not allow for the civilian agencies of the US government to take advantage of the off-the-shelf security in numerous products. Those standards require that these agencies attempt to purchase non-existent Clipper products or pursue a difficult waiver process, which is frequently discouraged by NSA.

Through advocacy, Mr. Bidzos has also made significant contributions. He is a member of the Boards of Directors of EPIC, the Electronic Privacy Information Center. EPIC is a major force in protecting individual rights to privacy in cyberspace, and has enjoyed financial, political, and technical support from Mr. Bidzos since the early 1990's. Mr. Bidzos has been a tireless advocate for privacy rights, testifying before the house and senate several times on behalf of the U.S. computer industry, and has given hundreds of talks and speeches around the world.

June 18, 1997

To whom it may concern:

For the fiscal years 1995, 1996, and 1997 (as of June 18, 1997), RSA has received the following cash amounts from the stated federal agencies:

US Department of Labor	$310 in 1995
NASA	$605 in 1995
Ministry of Defense	$ 90 in 1995
Department of Foreign Affairs & International Trade	$608.38 in 1995
US Department of Labor	$310 in 1995

No other amounts are known as received from federal government agencies during the above stated period for either RSA Data Security, Inc. or D. James Bidzos, President, personally.

Sincerely,

Kathryn K. Conrow
Chief Financial Officer

Mr. BRADY. Thank you, Mr. Bidzos. And, as we pass the mike to Mr. Rotenberg, I will yield the chair to our Chairwoman. Thank you.

Mrs. MORELLA. Mr. Brady did a terrific job. Mr. Rotenberg, we look forward to hearing your testimony.

STATEMENT OF MARC ROTENBERG, DIRECTOR, ELECTRONIC PRIVACY INFORMATION CENTER, AND ADJUNCT PROFESSOR, GEORGETOWN UNIVERSITY LAW CENTER, WASHINGTON, DC

Mr. ROTENBERG. Thank you very much, Madam Chairwoman. And, thank you to the Subcommittee for the chance to be here this morning.

I haven't been involved with cryptography for quite as long as some of the other members on the panel, but I was there at the birth of the Computer Security Act 10 years ago. And, I would like to say just a few words about this piece of legislation.

You know that at that time in the late 1980's, we didn't have the Internet, we didn't have the World Wide Web. There was not much commercial use of cryptography outside of the financial services sector.

And, we were, at the same time, very much concerned about the Soviet acquisition of western technology. Nonetheless, Congress, through bipartisan support, recognized the need to give NIST a primary role in the development of technical standards to protect computer security within the Federal Government and to create a process for openness, public accountability and private sector participation as those decisions were made.

Now, there have been some bumps in the road over the last 10 years. The Memorandum of Understanding, which was signed in 1989, I think took us on an unfortunate detour.

And, there have been a couple of technical standards discussed earlier—the escrowed encryption standard and the DSS, which have also created some problems. Nonetheless, the fundamental purpose of this legislation, I think, has stood the test of time.

What H.R. 1903 would do is strengthen the Computer Security Act of 1987, build on a solid foundation and ensure that computer security standards are responsive to the needs of the civilian agencies and make best use of private sector input and public advice. And, I can't stress just quite how urgent this is today, 10 years later, because today, in fact, we are increasingly dependent upon the Internet and the World Wide Web for all of the commercial activities and opportunities and electronic commerce that you've heard discussed earlier.

And, we are, at the same time, very much aware of the computer security risks that people face today on line. If you look at some of the recent opinion polls of computer users, what are they most concerned about? Privacy is right up there at the very top.

And, they are talking about their information in computer systems, in the Federal Government's computer systems. And, you know we have legislation that protects that information. But, without the technical standards that ensure that the systems are secure, it's not enough.

What H.R. 1903 does, then, is to ensure that private sector leadership will continue to play a critical role in the development of these standards. It will strengthen the Computer Systems Security and Privacy Advisory Board—I would like to say the island of sanity in the realm of computer security decision-making, that for anyone who has done some work with the board—and I've been there many times over the last 5 or 6 years and continue to be impressed by the very thoughtful, collaborative effort that the board has undertaken to get public input, the best technical advice and ensure that that's incorporated into decision-making.

H.R. 1903 strengthens the Advisory Board. And, I think this is very good.

Also, I would like to say just a word on Section 7. A couple of the witnesses earlier raised some concerns that perhaps Section 7 would be putting NIST in the job of doing some things it shouldn't be doing.

Section 7 actually, I think, is critical to the success of this legislation, because what Section 7 does is require the Department of Commerce to take note of the foreign availability of strong encryption products before the Secretary of Commerce is able to make decisions and recommendations on policy in this area. This is only, you know, common sense.

I mean, obviously these are contentious issues and different groups have different views about what the significance is of foreign availability. But, without some mechanism within the Federal Government to make sure that that information is available to policy makers, I think many of the decisions in this area will continue to be made with blinders on. And, that's not a good way to make policy.

Finally, if I could make just one brief recommendation regarding the proposed study for the National Research Council. As you may know, the NRC completed last year a very well regarded study on cryptography policy, a very complex issue, a comprehensive review and well received. And, I think they've done a good job and should continue to work in the area of computer security.

My only question, which I would like to raise at this point, is whether perhaps topics outside of public key management might also be considered. And, specifically this means looking at new techniques to promote privacy and security on line, techniques to promote anonymous or pseudo-anonymous commerce and communications that are now being explored in other countries.

I think this is also an important area of opportunity and growth for us. And, perhaps the NRC would look in this area as well.

But, speaking on behalf of a lot of people who are using the Internet today and concerned with privacy and security issues, I can tell you that H.R. 1903 is a very important step forward in the right direction. It builds on a solid foundation.

And, we would be happy to provide whatever support we can to move this along. Thank you.

[The prepared statement of Mr. Rotenberg follows:]

Testimony and Statement for the Record of

Marc Rotenberg
Director, Electronic Privacy information Center
Adjunct Professor, Georgetown University Law Center

on the Computer Security Enhancement Act of 1997,
H.R. 1903

Before the House of Representatives,
Committee on Science,
Subcommittee on Technology

June 19, 1997

Electronic Privacy Information Center
666 Pennsylvania Ave., SE
Suite 301
Washington, DC 20003
202 544 9240 (tel)
202 547 5482 (fax)
http://www.epic.org

My name is Marc Rotenberg. I am the Director of the Electronic Privacy Information Center (EPIC), a public policy research organization in Washington, DC that focuses on emerging privacy and civil liberties issues. I am also on the faculty at Georgetown University Law Center where I have taught a course on the Law of Information Privacy since 1991. With me this morning is Shauna Van Dongen and Shamir Merali, who have assisted me in the preparation of this testimony. I appreciate the opportunity to appear before the subcommittee this morning to comment on the Computer Security Enhancement Act of 1997 (CSEA).

The CSEA is an important piece of legislation whose urgency is underscored by the fact that many of the aspirations of the Computer Security Act of 1987[1] still remain to be realized. That law recognized the critical importance of developing security standards that are compatible with the needs of civilian agencies within the federal government and of commercial development in the private sector. The original Computer Security Act made clear that the best and most robust technical standards would result from open government procedures, active public input, and the advice of the best technical experts.

This morning, I will briefly review the significant developments since passage of the Computer Security Act. I will then focus on four important aspects of the CSEA and will also make some recommendations as to how it could be strengthened further. I should also say at the outset that of all the bills now before Congress on the difficult and sometimes contentious issues of computer security, the Computer Security Enhancement Act of 1997 is the most thoughtful, well reasoned, and forward-looking measure. I would like to commend the Subcommittee and the original cosponsors for your efforts.

<u>Summary</u>

First, the CSEA emphasizes private sector leadership in the development of technological solutions to data security and privacy problems. The use of existing private sector technologies is encouraged, as is the development by the private sector of new technologies. This is a positive step which recognizes that standard-setting and guidelines should be a cooperative effort between the appropriate government agencies and the private sector.

Second, the CSEA strengthens the role of the Computer System Security and Privacy Advisory Board. The Advisory Board has played a pivotal role, since passage of the CSA, in providing public input into the

---

[1] P.L. 100-235.

decision-making process. It is appropriate to build on the success of the Board and ensure that it continues to have the resources necessary to evaluate important concerns about computer security and privacy.

Third, the CSEA recognizes that that the United States is not grappling with the issues of data security and privacy in a vacuum. The Act provides a mechanism whereby U.S. decision-makers can take into account the public availability of encryption technologies outside of the U.S. when formulating U.S. policy on encryption. I hope that an awareness of technologies available outside the United States will influence decision-makers to adopt a policy on encryption that will help U.S. computer hardware and software manufacturers to be competitive in what is essentially a global market.

Fourth, the CSEA strengthens the role of NIST. It encourages NIST to evaluate technical evidence and to develop standard procedures and tests for encryption. Most importantly, the Act places a duty on NIST to report on these technical issues to the public. The new requirements of accountability in the development of computer technologies should go a long way toward achieving one of the Computer Act of 1987s goals of transparency.

A Brief Overview of Information Security on Federal Computer Systems

There is a vast amount of personal information stored on government computer systems. There are legal standards, such as the Privacy Act, to protect this information, but this is not enough. Our concern is that this information be secure, to ensure that there is no breach of personal privacy. The best way to ensure security is to promote rapid and open development of information security technology. That is to say, openness and public accountability promotes good science, and good science accelerates the development of superior systems. This was the intent of the original Computer Security Act, which was a response to a misplaced emphasis on national security and information classification.

In 1984, the president signed a National Security Decision Directive, the NSDD 145, which assigned significant responsibility for the security of government security systems to the Department of Defense, specifically to the National Security Agency (NSA).[2] In particular, this executive directive gave the NSA the task of protecting "sensitive, but classified" information; the NSDD145 gave the intelligence agency broad authority to peruse computer databases for such information.

---

[2] "National Policy on Telecommunications and Automated Information Systems Security" (September 17, 1984).

In response to widespread concerns about an intelligence agency having such broad responsibility over non-classified information, Congress enacted the Computer Security Act of 1987 (CSA). The CSA assigned responsibility for developing information security policy and guidelines to the National Bureau of Standards (now, the National Institute of Standards and technology -- NIST). Congress recognized that good technology is indispensable to the growth of security systems. NSA-imposed restrictions stifle innovation, and chill the vigorous research and development that goes on the academic community, and in the private computer industry.

Government participation in the growth of security has had a substantial impact on the private sector: The Data Encryption Standard (DES), after being adopted by the NBS in 1977, quickly became the worldwide industry standard after being adopted by the American National Standards Institute.[3]

By enacting the CSA, Congress sought to remove restraints on technological innovation in the private sector. Congress intended to provide a statutory mandate for a strong security program headed up by NIST. Congress responded to the central issue of whether responsibility for the security and privacy of information stored in government computer systems ought to be entrusted to a civilian or intelligence agency by giving NIST the mandate to "develop[] standards, guidelines and associated methods and techniques for computer systems". Congress recognized that in the "interest of national defense or foreign policy", some federal computer systems should be subject to NSA security guidelines, and went to great lengths to spell out which systems should be outside the ambit of NIST's statutory mandate.

Unfortunately, in 1989 NIST and the NSA signed a Memorandum of Understanding (MOU) which set the stage for many of the problems which followed. Among other things, the MOU

- transferred authority to establish and review computer standards from NIST to the NSA;

- created a Technology Working Group to review computer security issues;

- created a new layer of national security review, to be carried out by the NSA;

---

[3] See David Sobel, "Governmental Restrictions on the Development and Dissemination of Cryptographic Technologies: The Controversy over the Digital Signature Standard," in Computer Law Reporter, Volume 16, Number 2 (1992).

- invited the NSA to, "upon request by Federal agencies, their contractors and other government sponsored entities, conduct assessments of the hostile intelligence threat to federal information systems, and provide technical assistance and recommend endorsed products for application to secure systems against the threat;" and

- granted NSA the authority to review all matters of cryptography undertaken by NIST.

The problems with this arrangement quickly became apparent with the development of the Digital Signature Standard (DSS), a technique to enable authentication and promote electronic commerce. The DSS was developed by NIST, with significant technical help from the NSA, which "evaluated and provided candidate algorithms, including one eventually selected by NIST". DSS was widely criticized as a "flawed standard" and one that is "inferior" to rival technologies developed in the private sector.

The problems with the DSS resulted from ambiguity in the relationship between the NSA and NIST during the development of the standard. There have been calls for revisions to DSS, to be carried out more openly. We are pleased that that the Computer System Security and Privacy Advisory Board recently recommended the consideration of additional algorithms. Nonethelees, the experience with the DSS confirms our belief that the best technological development is driven by openness and public accountability. This belief is further strengthened by the Advanced Encryption Standard (AES) story.

A process to develop AES was recently announced by NIST.[4] NIST announced that as a first step in the process, it would publish for comment its criteria for the new standard, and would solicit candidate encryption algorithms for submission. One may conclude that NIST has recognized, as we have and continue to believe strongly, that openness rather than secrecy will best serve its needs as it develops this piece of important technology.

NIST should be commended for pursuing procedures for the development of this technical standard that are most closely aligned with commercial needs and the expertise of the technical community. Nonetheless, we believe that passage of the Computer Security Enhancement Act is necessary to ensure that future standard-setting follows the approach exemplified by the AES rather than the DSS.

<u>Impact of enhanced Private Sector input on Information Security technology</u>

---

[4]   Federal Register: January 2, 1997 (Volume 62, Number 1).

The CSEA will extend the role of the private sector by recognizing cryptography technology exists and can be provided by private sector companies to deal with issues of security, identification and privacy for both government and private activities. (Sec. 2(a)(3)). The CSEA also recognizes that market forces, not government, are a key factor in development and use of encryption technologies. (Sec. 2(a)(4)). Most importantly, the CSEA asks the NISTto assist, and not direct, the development of voluntary standards for Public Key Management Infrastructure. The bill says that upon the request of the private sector, NIST is to aid in establishing voluntary interoperable standards and guidelines to help in the establishment of non-Federal management infrastructures for public keys that can be used to communicate with and conduct transactions with the Federal Government. (Section 3(2)) Finally, the CSEA asks NIST to actively promote the use of commercially available products to provide for security and privacy of sensitive information in Federal computer systems. (Section 5(c)).

The CSEA also helps ensure that NIST is less likely to be swayed by improper influence in the development of technical standards. The bill focuses on improving computer security as the measure for evaluating agency participation and makes clear that NIST's reliance on NSA guidelines should be permissive rather than mandatory. (Sections 9(1)(2)).

These sections together will help ensure that NIST cooperates with the private sector in the development of technical standards that are appropriate for civilian and commercial applications. They provide for an external, non government perspective which is likely to inject positive and dynamic input from the private sector. These sections allow U.S. computer firms to seek to develop innovative technical solutions to security and privacy problems.

<u>A Stronger Computer System Security and Privacy Advisory Board</u>

We are particularly pleased to see provisions in the CSEA that would strengthen the role of Computer System Security and Privacy Advisory Board. The Board has played a critical role since passage of the Computer Security Act, and continues to provide the critical link between the public user community and the agency.

The bill would require NIST to seek the advice of the Computer System Security and Privacy Advisory Board on standards and guidelines that are being considered for submission to the Secretary of Commerce and requires NIST to include a copy of the Advisory Board's recommendations with its submission. (Section 6(d)(1)).

The bill would also authorize funds for Advisory Board to identify issues related to computer security, privacy and cryptography and to convene public meetings, seek input and publish information on those subjects. (Section 6(d)(2)).

These provisions will help ensure that the best technical advice is made available to the Secretary and that resources will be available to the Board to continue its work set out in the statute.

<u>Encryption as an International Issue</u>

As you are no doubt aware, one of the most contentious issues in the realm of computer security is the question of encryption policy. There are strong views on all sides of the debate. My own organization has made clear its concerns about the various key escrow proposals that have been put forward by the Administration.

But whatever one's views may be of the best resolution of the encryption question, there should be no question that the provisions in the CSEA regarding the need to consider the availability of strong encryption products around the world is a necessary factor in the development of any sensible policy. It is simply not wise to base recommendations without consideration of the full range of relevant data.

The CSEA notes that Federal policy for control of the export of encryption technologies should be determined in light of the public availability of comparable encryption technologies outside of the United States. (Section 2(a)(5)). The CSEA says simply that if the Secretary of Commerce has imposed or might impose export restrictions on encryption technology, NIST may accept technical evidence from commercial providers to show that encryption technologies generally available outside the US provide stronger protection for privacy of computer data and transmissions of information in digital form than the encryption technologies incorporated in the commercial provider's product. (Section 7(e)(1)).

These sections require the Secretary to consider all of the relevant technical data in developing policies for encryption technology. This is especially important given the ease with which electronic information crosses geographical borders via the Internet and given the rapid growth of this technology.

<u>NIST's Reporting Role, Transparency and Public Accountability</u>

Critical also to the effective work of the NIST in this area is the need to report publicly on the developments that may affect the formulation of policy and commercial products.

The CSEA will require that NIST evaluate the technical evidence and report to House and Senate Committees and the Secretary of Commerce as well as develop standard procedures and tests for determining the capabilities of encryption technologies. NIST must provide information on those tests and procedures to the public. (Section 7(2)-(3)).

These sections establish an important public reporting duty for NIST regarding encryption technologies and will further development of open standards and policies that will promote public confidence.

<u>Recommendations</u>

I would like to comment briefly on section 12 of the CSEA which calls on the National Research Council to pursue a study of Public Key Infrastructure. I am pleased to see the NRC once again asked to review important matters of computer security. The last NRC report in this area was widely regarded for its comprehensive examination of a difficult and politically charged topic.[5]

At the same time, it is my hope that the NRC will turn its expertise to issues more specifically related to the development of privacy and security techniques for the Internet. Specifically, it is very important for the NRC to look at privacy enhancing technologies that may enable the growth of electronic commerce on the Internet and strengthen public confidence in Internet communication. Similar work has been carried in out in other countries, but the United States has still not looked closely at the significant opportunities that such technologies a provide. A report from the National Research Council, setting out the basic research and policy issues with some preliminary recommendations, would be very useful.

<u>Conclusion</u>

Computer security is obviously one of the crucial issues facing the public and federal agencies today. We believe that the National Institute of Standards and Technology has an important role to play in examining these problems and making recommendations. The Computer Security Enhancement Act creates a framework that will ensure a responsive, open decision-making process that will promote technical standards compatible with the interests of the civilian agencies and the commercial sector. H.R. 1903 is smart, sensible legislation.

---

[5] Cryptography's Role in Securing the Information Society (1996).

<u>References</u>

Souce documents, reports, and analysis of computer security issues and cryptography policy may be found at the EPIC web site:

Computer Security - http://www.epic.org/security/

Cryptography Policy - http://www.epic.org/crypto/

Marc Rotenberg is director of the Electronic Privacy Information Center, a public interest research organization in Washington, DC. He teaches information privacy law at Georgetown University Law Center. He was counsel to the Senate Judiciary Committee in 1987-1988 when the Computer Security Act was enacted. He has served on numerous national and international advisory panels, including most recently the Expert Panel on Cryptography Policy for the OECD. He has testified before Congress on many issues, including access to information, encryption policy, computer security, and privacy protection. He is a graduate of Harvard College and Stanford Law School.

In accordance with the rules of the House Science Committee, it is noted that neither Marc Rotenberg nor the Electronic Privacy Information Center have received any Federal grant or contract during the current or the two preceding fiscal years for work in the filed of computer security.

Mrs. MORELLA. Thank you, Mr. Rotenberg, for that. And, we are considering the concept of new techniques and would look forward to working with you on that.

I think what I will do for the—before we go to vote, maybe for the first round of questioning, I will—since I was out for a bit—as a courtesy, defer to Mr. Gordon for any questions.

Mr. GORDON. Thank you. We are on a tight framework here with a vote. And, I have a 5-minute rule just like you do.

And, so let me pose a question to you. And, then what I would like is for anyone on the Committee that would like to address it to crisply make some suggestions and then follow up with any kind of written comments that you would like.

Some States have begun to establish a legal framework for digital signatures. What, if any, should be the federal role to encourage the development of such requirements concerning the development of uniform standards or procedures for the certification authorities for this digital signature?

So, we will just start with anybody to make some quick comments. And, then I would like for you to follow up with any maybe written comments.

Mr. BIDZOS. I would be happy to offer one short answer to that question. You are correct, in that there are a number of efforts in various States. Utah has a Digital Signature Act, a number of States, to legitimize, identify and standardize the use of this digital signature technology. A number of private companies are working with a lot of local and state governments to do this.

I talked earlier about the different standards in place in the Federal Government. Essentially, what this whole process has done is built a large wall between industry and the Federal Government.

And, that wall is causing a problem, in that the Federal Government isn't playing a role in that entire process. So, we run the risk of islands of incompatibility if we continue to pursue this.

In fact, recent legislation in the Senate would propose that standards and products built according to new specifications would supersede all these efforts of the States. I think we are headed down the wrong road that way.

So, what's happened is in the absence of a leadership role by NIST over the last few years, industry and state and local and Federal Governments are going their own way. And, I think what one of the benefits of H.R. 1903 is that it would force the Federal Government to come together with industry and with the state and local governments.

Mr. GORDON. Excuse me. Any other suggestions? Yes, sir.

Mr. WALKER. I find myself agreeing with Jim. There are a number of suggestions that have been made over the last year by folks in the Administration that there should be some public infrastructure that would be sanctioned somehow by the Administration. I find that a very depressing thought.

And, linking it to export control and things like that I think is a very wrong thing. It's difficult to see industry just drifting into a way of doing this. That's where we are headed.

But, given the history of what has been happening over the last 7 or 8 years with the Clipper, digital signature and all the rest of these things, I would rather see the Federal Government stay back out of this. If NIST can help industry coordinate its activities, that's fine.

I really oppose——

Mr. GORDON. I don't mean to be discourteous, but is there anybody else that would like to make a quick comment?

Yes, sir.

Mr. BACHULA. Congressman, the White House and the Department of Commerce, along with other federal agencies, have been working for some 6 months now with the National Governors' Association on an effort called the "U.S. Innovation Partnership." It's an attempt to sort of collaboratively work on some problems in technology in general.

In the area of electronic commerce, the States have identified an interest in a collaborative, sort of not top down process by which they could work with the Federal Government to arrive at common solutions, not have it dictated to them. But, they do—they are looking for ways to arrive at a common solution rather than 50 separate ones.

And, they also recognize that it's not just a question of a technology but very often cases of state law, since they have commercial codes that may need to be updated in this area.

Mr. GORDON. Thank you. I'm afraid my time has run. And, I will welcome any further comments that you might want to submit.

Thank you.

Mrs. MORELLA. Because we have another vote on the Floor, we are going to adjourn for 10 minutes. And, whatever member of the Majority side comes back first, I will let take the chair so that we can continue with the questioning.

Thank you for your patience.

[Brief Recess.]

AFTER RECESS

Mr. DAVIS (Presiding.) Thank you. Other members are in the middle of a vote, our second vote, to adjourn today on the House Floor. So, I'm the first one back.

I missed some of your testimony. I read some last night that we had in, but I had a markup of our D.C. Committee today. In fact, we took Mrs. Morella away.

But, I think I know enough to ask a few questions here. And, correct me if I've gone over some ground that you may have already covered.

Mr. Walker, let me just ask you at this point: I think you were saying that NIST's job in this isn't to do an evaluation but you could help and assist. If NIST isn't doing the evaluations, how are they going to know what kind of assistance to offer some of these other companies?

You know, which product is best and that kind of stuff if you are not in the evaluation process?

Mr. WALKER. This is a difficult situation that—because I am not at all opposed to this capability if it can exist. I am just fearful if NIST or the government can do this.

I am reminded of NIST in some other areas of its endeavors in the past where it was asked to comment on a particular commercial product, commented on what it thought was an honest appraisal of it and then came under great pressure from folks that were critical of that particular comment, whether it was right or wrong, and caused a lot of difficulty for the National Bureau of Standards in those days.

To the extent that they have backed off pretty much across the board, as I understand, in not doing qualitative evaluations of products, because they have a difficult time defending the findings when they are contrary to the—whatever the industry group was that asked for it. For example, with the Data Encryption Standard, the only test that NIST does is it, essentially, will take your supposed DES algorithm, put in a known key, grind it for a million times and see if you got the right answer. They will do that, but they won't comment any further on it.

What we are asking in this bill for them to do is actually go in and try to understand not only the qualities of products that where supposedly the person submitting it is willing to give them lots of background, but we are saying we've got to do it for foreign products where you don't have access to the information. All you can do is try to run the product and see what it does.

When all you can do is run the product and see what it does, you can comment on very specific tests that you might run—conformance tests. It's very difficult in security to determine the things that a product doesn't do or the things that it does wrong.

I think the Defense Department, in its computer security initiative over the last 15 years, has spent an enormous amount of energy trying to come up with criteria for evaluating how good computer systems are. And, as much as I had hoped that would be a successful effort, I think it is pretty much viewed now as a failed effort.

And, I'm afraid we may be launching this off on to another repeat of that which will take enormous resources and for which the results, people aren't going to be happy with.

Mr. DAVIS. But, is part of your concern the fact that NIST is working right now on a limited budget in terms of setting priorities? This may not——

Mr. WALKER. Well, of course, a limited budget is the beginning of the problem. But, I'm actually fearful that you may provide them an enormous budget and they will do the same thing that the DOD did with the trusted computer system evaluation criteria—create a huge bureaucracy of 300 people and still not produce results that are the kind of things that we all want.

We would love to have people be able to say, "Yes, this product is really good," or, "That product is really not good." But, whenever the government says that product is not very good, it suddenly makes the government subject to all kinds of attacks and, as I understand it, all kinds of pressure through various legislative processes and elsewhere to, "Oh, no, amend your comment, because it's not favorable to my constituent," or whatever. And, that's the situation that I don't think we want to get an organization like NIST into.

Mr. DAVIS. All right, thank you. Let me ask Mr. Bidzos if he has any comment on that?

Mr. BIDZOS. I disagree with Steve on this. I think NIST would not be so ambitious, because I think they would understand that it would be counterproductive.

Let me use an analogy. What we don't want to do is if we are talking about cars instead of encryption, we don't want to ask NIST to decide which car is better, because Steve is right, people, you know, they are going to start thinking about how comfortable the seats are, how do the brakes feel. That's not what we are about.

The analogy I am talking about here is, let's say, that U.S. car makers sold products overseas but a government restriction caused them to limit the car speed to 40 miles an hour. And, then we found out that a foreign company was selling an upgrade kit that made the car go 120 again, like the ones sold in the United States.

The question is: Does the car overseas, after the upgrade kit is added, go 120 or not? We are asking NIST to operate a radar gun, not to evaluate whether they like the car or whether it's as good as American cars.

And, if the answer is that there's an industry that U.S. government policy is creating that exists for no reason other than to fill the void left by export policy, if the Commerce Department isn't going to help us understand that problem, who is?

Whose job is it to protect U.S. industry in that case if not the Commerce Department?

And, I think the funding provided by H.R. 1903 would address this problem, would give NIST the authority, the money to go and do this job. And, I think they are smart enough not to go off and pursue things that don't make sense, especially when there's ample history through the Defense Department that it's just not a good thing to do.

Mr. DAVIS. Let me ask—I will give you a chance, Mr. Walker, but let me just ask Mr. Bachula, in your testimony you noted that the key technology focus areas in the NIST security program, I think the third one you had was to provide objective criteria for testing and assessing the functionality and assurance of security technology in products.

And, just to bring you into this a little bit, isn't that something NIST ought to already be doing?

Mr. BACHULA. It's important to look at all the words in that sentence—objective criteria for testing but not to do the actual product testing. NIST is not an underwriter's laboratory. It's not a consumer's report.

We are a step removed from that. There are many private sector entities—and I'm talking now about the broad area of standards testing, the measurements—that provide the sort of direct services to American industry.

We are a step removed from that. We maintain basic units of measurements, derive units.

The standards and calibrations have to be traceable back to NIST. But, we are not in the actual product testing business. And, I don't think we want to be. And, good reasons have been expressed for that here.

Mr. DAVIS. Mr. Bachula, let me just add, Section 7, as I read it right now, doesn't impact the export control of encryption products.

However, I think Congress is going to certainly roll over the Administration on an encryption policy.

You saw the Judiciary vote. And, I think that will be a done deal, and I wouldn't be surprised if the Administration reversed it.

That's above your pay grade, I guess, as this goes.

Mr. BACHULA. It's outside the purview of——

Mr. DAVIS. Right.

Mr. BACHULA. (continuing) —NIST at this point.

Mr. DAVIS. But, do you believe that by simply quantifying the strength of foreign encryption products you would harm national security?

Mr. BACHULA. I think what we have right now is an existing process, an existing regulatory process, existing Executive Branch rulings on how we evaluate export controls. This would have the effect of putting NIST in the middle of that process and, essentially, second-guessing other agencies.

It's not a role we welcome. It has been suggested here that it's not perhaps a role we could do well.

And, the kinds of resources that it might ultimately require raise a question of priorities. We can serve a far better role in this general area and not get into that business.

Mr. DAVIS. Let me ask—and, Mr. Walker, I will give you a chance to comment in a second. But, I haven't heard from a couple of the other panelists.

Let me ask Mr. Rotenberg, if you have any comments on this?

Mr. ROTENBERG. Yes, Congressman. You know, the Department of Commerce already plays a significant role in cryptography policy. I don't think there's any question about that.

What Section 7 of this bill tries to do is make sure that the role that they play is based on some solid evidence, which I think is good not only for science but also for public policy. Basically, it says if you are going to make some recommendations about cryptography in the United States, you really have to take note of what's available around the world.

And, I think this is, you know, just a baseline. I mean, you may come down somewhere else and you may still have some disagreements.

But, I really do have to disagree with Mr. Bachula on this point. I think that's a critical role for NIST to play.

Mr. DAVIS. Okay. Yes, Mr. Diffie, you haven't said anything yet.

Mr. DIFFIE. Well, I find myself torn, because I'm inclined to agree——

Mr. DAVIS. You are going to break the tie up here. I think it's 2 to 2.

Mr. DIFFIE. I'm inclined to agree with the objectives of the section, but I'm inclined to think that people have underestimated the difficulty of this activity.

Three years ago before the Senate, Admiral John McConnell, Director of NSA, said a wonderful thing. He said, "I do a market survey of the world's cryptography every 24 hours."

Now, I think that's (a) true; and, (b) that you know how many billions of dollars they spend doing that. And, in some sense, evaluating cryptographic systems is the heart of cryptography and crypto analysis.

And, it's a very difficult job. And, I doubt that these resources are adequate to produce meaningful results to answer the kinds of issues that are being argued about in where you are saying, you know, "Is this just being exported into a market where there are equivalent products or are the products that are there not actually equivalent to this one?"

So, I am enthusiastic about the idea. I'm not capable of speaking for its success.

Mr. DAVIS. Mr. Walker, I want to give you another chance.

Mr. WALKER. Thank you. I appreciate it.

I agree completely with what was just said. I am in favor of the objectives of this. I am very concerned about how it gets done.

Let me give you some practical experience we've had. Back in 1993, just when Clipper came out, the Software Publishers Association and Professor Lance Hoffman and TIS got together and said, "Let's go out and see what foreign crypto is out there. Let's do a survey."

And, we have—we did that survey with those folks. We have kept it going. It is available on our Web page. It's updated every quarter. We have found thousands of foreign products and thousands of U.S. products.

I testified in both the fall of 1993 and in the spring of 1994 and brought in the foreign products that we had bought. And, there were—it was really neat, because the staffers, before the testimony, said, "Well, the Administration is telling us that there aren't any foreign products available." And, I was able to say, "Well, of course, there are. We have a list of all of these."

And, then they said, "Well, you can't buy them." And, then I was able to prove that we could buy them, because we had a stack of them.

And, then the question was, "Well, but they are not any good." And, the question was, "Are they any good? How do you use these?"

Well, some of them are, in fact, implementations of DES, for example, or of other algorithms. But, the tough problem with encryption products is key management. How do you manage the keys?

Some of them tell you to—these are little simple file encryption products that say, "Type in a pass code." Well, they use that pass code, then, to generate the key.

Well, they might generate a full 56-bit key or a 112-bit key. But, they might generate an 8-bit key or a 2-bit key. You don't know.

And, in fact, there have been allegations that some governments have influenced their companies in their countries to build flaws into systems that they might sell to the United States or elsewhere. It is very hard to know whether, in fact, there is a flaw in the key management system or perhaps even in the algorithm that you can't tell.

And, so I am concerned that asking NIST to—putting NIST in a position of being able to say that a particular product somewhere is better than some other product and making—having the government make a decision based on that, you are really going down a slippery slope very, very fast here.

Mr. ROTENBERG. Mr. Chairman——

Mr. DAVIS. Sure.

Mr. ROTENBERG. If I could just make one quick point.

Mr. DAVIS. Sure.

Mr. ROTENBERG. You know, my friend, Whit Diffie, I think, is right, that this is a difficult task, doing the evaluation. But, this is—the way this section is drafted is almost an appeal as a matter of right.

You see, what requires NIST to undertake this study is in the circumstance where the Secretary of Commerce has imposed or proposes to impose export restrictions on a product. So, here you have the U.S. government telling a U.S. firm, "You cannot send this product overseas." And, the U.S. firm simply wants to say, "Well, would you at least consider the fact that a similar product is currently available overseas?"

What Section 7 does is basically say to the Department of Commerce, "If you are going to take that step, Mr. Secretary, you have to at least consider the fact that a similar product may already be available." And, I think this is very sensible, because if you don't do that you just give this blanket authority that I think, you know, is not sensible.

And, I think this is a critical piece of the bill, frankly.

Mr. DAVIS. Okay. Anybody else? Mr. Bidzos.

Mr. BIDZOS. Could I just add one more comment again?

Mr. DAVIS. Sure.

Mr. BIDZOS. I would take issue with Steve's comments and Whit's, because I think that things have changed so much in the last few years that it's not true anymore that it's that hard to measure things.

When you've got companies who are exploiting our export control laws by doing nothing other than specifically replacing that small crypto part, representing as a part of the product a small—yes, complex but a small part, the review process is very manageable.

Also, when I testified before Senate Burns' committee last summer, I brought along with me a couple of chips, encryption chips, manufactured by NTT, the world's largest company. All these things that Steve was talking about—how do you generate keys and pass codes, maybe it's 2-bits—it's all in the chip. It works.

This is a $200 billion a year company that sells hundreds of millions of chips a year, and it knows how to make them. And, they work. And, there is nothing wrong with them. It's very easy to point to them and say, "These work."

This is an argument that has been put forth by other parts of the government, which is that, you know, you are not threatened competitively because the other products aren't as good. It is easy to demonstrate now that those products are as good.

And, as Marc points out, all we want to do is understand whether that's true or not. If you tell NIST that what they are going to do is take the money provided by H.R. 1903, go to Section 7 and duplicate what NSA tried to do in the 1980's and 1990's, sure, they are going to fail.

If you tell them that they are going to do an evaluation as comprehensive as NSA does when it attacks a crypto system it identifies, sure, they are going to fail. That is absolutely not what Section 7 asks NIST to do.

Mr. DAVIS. I think the last study on foreign availability is now 2 years old, and it was done by NIST.

Let me just ask one other question just to stir it up a little bit. Do you think that—what would be the result of a federal policy that divests NIST of its jurisdiction and gives these duties to NSA?

Mr. WALKER. I think I can speak for all of us in saying that would be a total disaster.

Mr. DAVIS. Okay. Does everybody agree with that?

Mr. BIDZOS. I think you would have a situation where an agency of the Defense Department is making economic policy. So, maybe that's the right question.

Is it okay for NSA to continue making economic policy? And, I submit the answer is no.

Mr. DAVIS. Actually, I appeared on a panel with Mr. Magaziner and a group of high technology executives. And, he just said, "I agree with you on encryption, but the NSA boys won this battle." So, maybe they are making policy.

I am going to turn it over now to Chairwoman Morella and let her assume her Chairwoman's role. Connie.

Mrs. MORELLA. Well, gentlemen, we are finally reaching the finale. And, I appreciate your patience in being here and going through this, particularly the contributions that you have made to our understanding of this bill.

We may disagree with a couple of you on Section 7, but I think we can work out those problems. And, I appreciated Mr. Davis asking some of those questions and your responses.

I guess, Mr. Rotenberg, I wanted to ask you what is your appraisal or assessment of encryption standard setting efforts outside of the United States?

And, do you think we properly address that in this bill, H.R. 1903?

Mr. ROTENBERG. Well, I appreciate your question. I spent the past year working with the Organization for Economic Cooperation and Development on the framework for international cryptography policy.

And, what struck me, looking at how other governments were dealing with this issue, is how important it was to ensure that the Departments of Commerce and Trade and Telecommunications played an active role in this technical standard-setting arena, because I think as other governments realize today, you know, this is the future. And, these technologies are the technologies that are going to make possible commerce in the 21st Century.

So, my sense, having watched these developments in other countries is that today the need to strengthen our commercial side, civilian side, policy development is critical. And, I think in that respect, H.R. 1903 is, you know, absolutely on course.

It is the direction that I think that countries which are aware of the need to ensure strong and vibrant economies are taking.

Mrs. MORELLA. I think I saw you nodding affirmatively. And, I guess that means that you are in favor of his response, that we do need that comes out in H.R. 1903?

Mr. BIDZOS. Yes.

Mrs. MORELLA. I guess, you know, we've tried to focus on enhancing the Computer Security Act and not to be overwhelming.

And, I guess, by and large, do you think we have done a good job with this bill?

Now, I think Mr. Rotenberg does, Mr. Bidzos does. Mr. Walker does?

Mr. WALKER. Yes.

Mrs. MORELLA. Okay. You are now on record. Okay, very good. And, I just wanted——

Mr. WALKER. I think this is a very good bill. There are a few parts of it I think need to be looked at.

But, I agree completely with what you are saying and what is trying to be accomplished here.

Mrs. MORELLA. If you can give to this Subcommittee whatever your recommendations are, if there is some language within it that you think might be——

Mr. WALKER. Well, that was part of the testimony that was——

Mrs. MORELLA. That you have in it. So, you have given us that.

Mr. WALKER. And, I don't disagree. It's Section 7, I suppose, and also the section earlier, the new paragraph 6 somewhere, that says they should be evaluating products and all.

I'm just worried that, as my associates here have been saying, all Section 7 is doing is the following. Well, if that's all that Section 7 is doing, then I agree with it completely, too.

Mrs. MORELLA. Okay.

Mr. WALKER. My concern is that I was part of the government for 20 some years, and I've watched the government since then. And, when you say, "Go do this," they tend to say, "Oh, but in order to make sure I am doing it right, I have to do this and this and this." And, that turns into a gigantic situation, which is very expensive and ends up being unsatisfactory to anybody.

That's my real concern here, that whether you are telling— whether the language is clear enough that this is the only thing they are going to do I think is debatable, because we've come to different views just reading the words. My concern is that if it is not very clear how limited it is that you want them to do that you may be creating a gigantic bureaucracy.

That's really my concern here, not with the principle that is trying to be accomplished. We do need to understand how these systems work, both foreign and domestic.

I just find it hard—it has been hard up until now for people to do that. If it's all built into a chip, it's easy to test it.

But, a lot of these products involve a lot of software. There are threats that other governments have, in fact, directed companies to build flaws into these systems. I'm not going to mention specifics, but there have been these things in the press for some time. And, it's very hard to find out whether that's really true or not.

And, if you want NIST to be able to get into that level of detail, they won't succeed because no one else has. That's really—it's a matter of degree as opposed to whether the principle is there or not.

Mrs. MORELLA. I appreciate your statement and your concern about misinterpretation and taking on too much responsibility in that interpretation layers.

Mr. Rotenberg, I think you would like to respond to that.

Mr. ROTENBERG. Madam Chairwoman, there was some discussion on this point earlier. And, I'm actually very pleased at Steve Walker's comment.

I think if there is an understanding here about what the intent of Section 7 is—and I certainly take the section to mean simply that where the Secretary of Commerce is planning to impose some restriction through export control authority, it would be sensible to look at foreign availability. I think if we are in agreement on this point, then, you know, then maybe there is not really a problem here.

I think we are also in agreement on the complementary point, which is not the idea to do this sort of massive survey of everything on a real time basis. That would not be an appropriate role for NIST.

But, if the Secretary of Commerce is exercising export control authority, I think, you know, developers and firms and others, as a matter of right, should be able to say, "Listen, before you make this decision that affects me or my company, you know, please consider what is happening in other countries."

Mr. WALKER. I don't disagree with what you are saying. I think my real concern with Section 7—I don't have it in front of me—is the part that says 180 days after the bill is passed NIST will prepare criteria as to how all this will be done. Well, how far are we going to go?

I mean, do you have to understand whether the key management system really works and if there are any flaws in it? Because if you are going to say something is okay or good, I mean, this is—that's the part—it's really the second portion where it talks about creating these criteria and publishing them that's going to be the difficult thing to do.

If we can come up with those criteria and everybody can be happy with them, then the 30 days response to a particular product is fine. I have just watched government develop criteria for testing things for enough years now that I am fearful that is going to be a hard thing to do.

Mrs. MORELLA. I understand what you are saying. It's simply that if you stay away from any time frames, sometimes these things get lost. And, so that's the inclination.

There is also a possibility that in report language that would accompany this bill there could be a clarification, just, you know, a possibility that could be worked out, too.

But, I really didn't give you, Mr. Diffie, an opportunity to respond. I would like to very much.

Mr. DIFFIE. Well, I think that actually, in listening to this discussion, I am reminded that user trust in security systems is the bottom line problem and, in some sense, the most difficult problem in all of security. And, I am suddenly more enthusiastic than I was when I walked in that NIST should get its toe farther into this water as an issue of technology indirectly, not an issue—I think issues of intelligence policy and competition, you know, assignment of responsibility and all those things come up.

But, I think it is very important to see whether maybe old people like me are not stuck in our ways. And, I spoke while you were absent, saying, you know, I agreed with the objectives here, but I was worried that, after all, this is, in some sense, most of the activity of NSA, which is a multi-billion dollar activity.

And, so I despaired of doing it on a million dollar budget. But, I am beginning to think that, you know, there may be hidden requirement blocks there in my thinking and that it's definitely worth investigating whether this can be done in a way that will suit these objectives without getting ensnared in things that you didn't really need to do.

And, it wouldn't be the first time that I thought somebody was going to get ensnared and somebody had better footwork than I did and stepped around it.

Mrs. MORELLA. Oh, what an open-minded man. I appreciate that very much.

[Laughter.]

Mrs. MORELLA. And, now to Mr. Bachula. I would like to have you say the same thing that Mr. Diffie did.

[Laughter.]

Mr. BACHULA. Ms. Morella, your original question was did the Committee do a good job——

Mrs. MORELLA. Yes.

Mr. BACHULA. (continuing) —in drafting this bill.

[Laughter.]

Mr. BACHULA. And, let me say that I think this Committee always does a good job, particularly in its oversight of the Technology Administration and NIST.

[Laughter.]

Mr. BACHULA. I think that while we have discussed some portions of this bill and some issues that obviously bring out passion and strong views, we should not lose sight of the strong areas of agreement that we have among all of the witnesses here and with the Committee—a stronger role for NIST in the area of computer security, updating the Act to sort of match the times, emphasis on the voluntary consensus process, working with industry, arriving at federal standards that are consistent with commercial standards and not trying to have separate.

While there was some very, very good discussion about the history in this regard, I think that where we are today in our efforts to seek comment on the Advanced Encryption Standard, to modify the DSS, to move in those directions, most of the witnesses basically agree that where we are today and where we believe we are going is where we ought to be. So, we have vast areas of agreement, both among the witnesses and with the Committee on this bill.

And, the emphasis on a section or two shouldn't override that.

Mrs. MORELLA. Thank you. Just one final question and, again, to Mr. Bachula.

I wondered what, in your opinion, is the significance of the DES being broken yesterday?

Can you tell us what NIST's role was in developing this Data Encryption Standard, what the procedures were that NIST followed and what—maybe what input did NIST receive?

Mr. BACHULA. The DES standard, as you know, is some 20 years old. It has been highly successful.

It still works. I think it might be a disservice to consumers out there to think that somehow their ATM transactions are now threatened or that they can't use software to communicate with their bank.

The incident that was described in the "Wall Street Journal" today involved, at least according to the newspaper story—I mean, I don't have independent information—something like 10,000 people, 4 months of work, running through in sort of brute force the 72 quadrillion combinations that were needed to break the code. The normal hacker doesn't have that kind of capacity and capability.

At the same time, it does underscore the need for the Advanced Encryption Standard that we are working on in an open process with industry. So, the targets keep changing.

We are going to need to keep up with those changing technologies and are very much engaged in that process. But, I don't think that we want to have citizens frightened by today's newspaper story that they can't—that their money in the bank account is somehow going to be stolen.

Mrs. MORELLA. Did you want to comment on that, Mr. Bidzos, since you are sort of an expert on it?

Mr. BIDZOS. Thank you. I'm not sure I'm an expert, but I would like to make a couple of comments.

This reminds me of a conversation. Part of Mr. Bachula's response reminds me of a conversation I heard between a couple of military men who were talking about a particular place where U.S. soldiers were serving, and they were talking about the odds of being one of the casualties.

And, it was pretty remote. You know, your chances are something like one in 80,000 of being killed over in this place.

And, then one fellow said, "That's not bad." And, the other one said, "Well, unless you are that one in 80,000."

And, so as long as it's not your key, I guess it's okay. The problem is—the other problem is that 10,000 people out of the 80 million or 90 million who use the Internet worldwide is a ridiculously small number.

It can be done. It has been demonstrated that it can be done. It has to be taken seriously.

I think the more relevant comment is that I just think it's unfortunate—I commend NIST for the AES project. It's very important.

And, one of the many wonderful things about H.R. 1903 is that it provides the funding and the mandate for NIST to continue this effort. That is critically important.

I would just point out that it's—it may not be too late. It certainly isn't too soon.

But, we are—just having heard 48 hours ago about DES being broken, we are at the beginning of a process that's going to go for at least 1 or 2 years in getting a new encryption standard in place. I think this bill, with its provisions, in the future would prevent this from happening.

NIST would have the mandate and the money to think ahead, to look ahead, plan ahead. And, we wouldn't be in the position that we are in now.

Mrs. MORELLA. I am going to turn the meeting over to Congressman Ehlers to conclude it after his questioning, to adjourn it, and ask your permission that members who would like to submit questions to you may be able to do so, because we would very much like to do that.

I wanted to thank you all also for being here and continuing to follow through with us on H.R. 1903.

Mr. Ehlers.

Mr. EHLERS. Thank you, Madam Chairwoman. I suspect I could keep you here most of the afternoon with questions, but I won't do that because I have a 1 p.m. meeting and you would probably enjoy a break.

After hearing this loquacious panel, I decided one thing. Cryptographers are not cryptic, among other things.

[Laughter.]

Mr. EHLERS. And, I am really puzzled at the origin of that word. I will have to investigate that some time.

It doesn't have anything to do with cemeteries or mortuaries or your patterns of speech.

A couple of other side comments. Mr. Bachula, I don't know if you recall, but I was a member of the Michigan Legislature when you worked for Governor Blanchard. I suspect at that point neither of us expected to be sitting here facing each other in a room like this.

I suspect neither of us also expected that your boss, Governor Blanchard, would end up being in the same law firm as my friend, Senator Dole. So, life is full of funny coincidences.

On the issues of the day, I listened with interest to the discussions about Section 7 and the opinions, pro and con. And, one question, which any of you can answer, is if we remove the current export controls on encryption, do your problems with Section 7 go away? Obviously, it would have to be changed somewhat.

Mr. Bidzos.

Mr. BIDZOS. I would just like to save you a trip to the library, Mr. Ehlers.

Cryptography is made up of two Greek root words, krupto and graphia. Being a native Greek, I am particularly interested in that myself.

And, they translate, respectively, into English as secret writing.

Mr. EHLERS. I read that at one time. It slipped my mind, which happens as you get older. Thank you.

Your response to the question, Mr. Walker.

Mr. WALKER. Well, if the motivation for Section 7 is to be able to provide the response to U.S. companies when they are concerned about not being able to export their product, if a foreign product that's better is already out there, if the export controls went away, then you wouldn't need Section 7.

Whether we still would want the ability to have somebody assess the quality of different products out there, that need is always going to be there whether they are U.S. products or whether they are foreign products or whatever. And, it is that assessment of how good these things are that I remember well being asked by—before I testified here 3 or 4 years ago, we had bought a number of foreign products, and the question was just how good are they. And, it's very, very hard to figure that out.

So, the desire on the part of people to be told, "Yes, this product is good," or, "That product isn't good," is still going to be there even if export controls go away.

I suspect the incentive to push for Section 7 will go away if, in fact, the export controls are eliminated.

Mr. EHLERS. This need that you mentioned, would that be something that is worth government money being spent for?

Mr. WALKER. Yes. But, I hope it doesn't turn into the giant bureaucracy again.

I mean, the Defense Department had a problem—it still does—in the 1970's called the "Multilevel Security Problem." They were building computer systems around the world, and everyone who had access into the system had to have a top secret clearance because you couldn't trust the computer not to reveal top secret information to somebody with a lower clearance.

The WWMCCS system, which I was involved in when I was at the Pentagon, a huge problem. It's very expensive to clear everybody to a top secret level; and, yet, we couldn't trust the computers.

Well, I began—and a lot of people continued on—a substantial effort to figure out can we determine whether commercially available systems are good enough to be able to be used in an environment where top secret information can be there but people with a lower clearance can have access to it. In some sense, that's an easier problem than the one we are trying to deal with here.

And, the Defense Department wasn't able to do it. I mean, they tried hard. But, we have very—we still have the multilevel security problem today.

I hope that the wording of Section 7 can be done in such a way that it doesn't become another multilevel security problem. But, I have watched these things happen enough times in my career that I'm very fearful that what will happen is NIST will, if I'm right, and I may be wrong, invest a lot of energy in trying to build these criteria because you asked for in 180 days the criteria before this process actually goes into effect. And, they will fail. They won't quite get it right.

People won't be happy with it. And, 2 or 3 years down the line, you will have another hearing here and you will say, "Darn, you guys in NIST didn't do a good job at this," and you will chastise them and tell them to stop doing it or whatever.

And, I am just fearful we are going to go off on a wild goose chase here. It's not that the objectives of it aren't good and useful; and, it's not that if we can constrain it in some way that it can work.

My concern is that—and I saw this happen in the DOD process, we tried to come up with simple criteria and then people said, "Well, yes, but suppose somebody finds something wrong? Suppose I endorse something and somebody finds something wrong with it? I had better make those criteria a little bit stronger. I better try to ask for more." We called it "criteria creep." It was a technical term.

And, what happened is systems that were supposed to only be sort of good, suddenly the requirements for documentation and all became enormous. And, I'm just frightened of that process.

If we can do it short of that, then this is a good thing to do. It's probably a useful thing for the government to do even if export controls are eliminated.

Mr. EHLERS. Does anyone else wish to comment? Mr. Rotenberg.

Mr. ROTENBERG. Just briefly, Mr. Congressman. You asked the question if export controls were to go away would Section 7 be necessary. And, I think in some respects, the problem is anticipated that Section 7 would go away on its own accord, because the Secretary would not be exercising the authority. And, the need to conduct the evaluation would go away.

And, I think in this regard, as well, this is actually a very sensible provision. It basically says if you are going to exercise this authority and you do want to restrict the ability of U.S. firms to sell product overseas, then we need in place some mechanism.

And, I've been rereading the language. I actually think it's a very, sort of streamlined procedure that is described here in the legislation for creating the mechanism.

We need some mechanism to evaluate foreign availability. Now, if you choose not to exercise the authority, you know, it goes away.

But, as I said, it really—I hear Mr. Walker's concerns and it's, you know, not because I disagree with him that there could be scenarios in which this is, you know, expensive and bureaucratic. But, I really don't see it in the bill. That doesn't seem to be the intent.

And, I actually don't see the authority there for what you have described.

Mr. EHLERS. Other comments? Mr. Diffie.

Mr. DIFFIE. The—I think that the question being asked is what is the importance of a capability to evaluate security systems. And, I think the answer is that independent of its application to this particular case of judging export decisions that it is perfectly appropriate for NIST, as a body whose work is the development of the technology underlying standards, to be given the mandate to attempt to develop an adequate appraisal technology which will be applicable to many things from—they won't necessarily do the individual system evaluations once that technology has been developed, but in determining what you have to ask people about a proposed crypto system, for example, in order to be able to judge it against criteria at a reasonable cost.

I think that's something very, very appropriate to charge NIST with at the moment.

Mr. EHLERS. Mr. Bachula.

Mr. BACHULA. Sir, I think the testimony of the witnesses here has made it clear that there are two issues involved here. One is a NIST capability, which was just described, whether it should have it, what the resources would be, whether it could do it well, whether it's hard to do, whether it's easy to do. And, we have heard a variety of testimony on that subject matter.

The second question, though, is the provisions of this bill, which essentially modifies the existing regulatory process. And, that part of the bill, which puts NIST into a regulatory function, is what the Administration objects to.

It puts NIST, a non-regulatory agency, one that has never been in this business before, in the middle of a process of second-guessing other agencies' work. The question of foreign availability is one of the considerations that the existing regulatory process can consider.

This would seem to sort of raise the stakes on that issue. And, changing the existing regulatory process probably should be done in a different venue, not this bill.

Mr. EHLERS. I suspect—and I haven't been involved, heavily involved, in the writing, but I believe the intent was not to involve you in the regulatory process anyway. And, perhaps the staff would want to talk to you about the language, if that's your concern.

Mr. BACHULA. But, if you listened to some of the other witnesses today, that's exactly what they are applauding about, the provisions as they read it, because they think it would modify the process.

Mr. EHLERS. Mr. Walker, last comment.

Mr. WALKER. In trying to figure out how to move forward on this, I seem to be the one that is bringing up technical objections here.

I think one of the strengths of the bill that may get us out of this if you proceed with Section 7 as it is, the Advisory Board. Having the Advisory Board role strengthened so that it can be involved in this, I think, would be an excellent way to try to ensure that the concerns I have of what might go wrong in building a bureaucratic process and all can be held in sway.

I mean, it's the kind of thing you all can't look at on a yearly basis or every 2 years or whatever, but the Advisory Board could. And, to the effect that the provisions of the bill strengthen the role of the Advisory Board and maybe in the documents that accompany the bill you can say, "Hey, Advisory Board, keep a close eye on Section 7 so that it doesn't turn into a bureaucratic nightmare." And, it may be just exactly the kind of thing that Marc and I could agree would be a good way to proceed.

Mr. EHLERS. Thank you. Mr. Bidzos, do you have any comments? You haven't had an opportunity yet.

Mr. BIDZOS. I would just like to point out, with all due respect to Mr. Bachula, that NIST is now in the business of regulating the encryption industry because of its recently assumed responsibility for the export of cryptography recently handed to it from the State Department by the Administration—I'm sorry, the Commerce Department.

But, it seems to me that what H.R. 1903 is proposing to do is to say, "Gee, if that's going to be your job, then here are some funds with which you can conduct some investigation and research that should help you do it better."

And, you know, I feel Steve's pain. I mean, it's pretty clear that he had a very, very painful experience in the government before. But, that doesn't mean we shouldn't let NIST try to do it.

And, in one sense, just because NSA has been doing many of the things that the Computer Security Act envisioned NIST doing doesn't mean that we should assume that NIST, if we correct that, will now try to do all of the things that NSA tried to do.

Mr. EHLERS. Thank you. I appreciate those comments. Just a few other quick questions.

Mr. Bachula, you referred at one point during the discussion—and I don't recall exactly in reference to which aspect of the bill—a concern about the need to build up additional expertise whether—maybe I'm putting words in your mouth. But, you seem to be concerned about NIST being able to handle some of the functions that we are assigning to it here.

One question I just wanted to ask: Do you have contact with the NSA? Do they make available to you any of their expertise?

Obviously, they seem to have one of the world's greatest collections of cryptographic experts. Are they, by charter, not allowed to help you out or advise you?

Mr. BACHULA. I think they have an awesome set of skills. In terms of basics or technical expertise, NIST has access to NSA and other experts around the government, as does the regulatory body, the Bureau of Export Administration, which is the part of the Department of Commerce that right now deals with export regulations. They have access to the same kind of expertise.

And, in terms of foreign availability and these kinds of determinations that are being talked about, they do it now in that avenue.

But, NIST has had a long relationship—some of it was described in the earlier history today—with NSA. And, again, they have many resources.

One question about resources, which was raised by another witness, was how much would it take to do the job. And, I can't cite the dollars spent by NSA in this area, but I can tell you that it—we could replace NIST with the order of magnitude.

Mr. EHLERS. I suspect you are probably right on that. In Section 12, I notice there is a call for another NRC study.

And, I am wondering, first of all, what the opinion of the panel is on that. Is that necessary?

And, second, are any aspects of the previous NRC study on this topic, even though directed at something else specifically, that would be useful on this particular topic?

Are there any comments on that? Mr. Rotenberg.

Mr. ROTENBERG. Mr. Congressman, I mentioned briefly in my testimony, first of all, that the NRC did very good work this past year in their report on computer security. I think that was very thoughtful, very comprehensive and well regarded.

And, I think it is an enormous resource to the Federal Government, the National Research Council.

I propose specifically in my testimony that it may be appropriate for the NRC to begin looking at what are sometimes termed "privacy enhancing technologies," ways to protect individual privacy, to promote commerce on line. There's obviously a great deal of interest in public key management. And, there may be some way to combine them.

But, this area, as well, I think is particularly important for users on the Internet today and is something the NRC would probably do a very good job with.

Mr. EHLERS. Thank you. Any other comments? Mr. Walker.

Mr. WALKER. I also believe that the NRC study that was concluded last year was very helpful. And, it was a comprehensive look across the board and made some of the best suggestions that have been made by the best learned bodies at the time.

And, in fact, a number of those folks were cleared and were able to participate in briefings from NSA and others and were able to come back and say that those concerns of, "Well, it's classified and I can't tell you," are not worth the arguments that are being made. And, I thought that was a major contribution that panel made. And, so I'm not against NRC panels.

I do believe that public key infrastructure is an issue where industry is really taking the lead and needs to take the lead. And, I am, in fact, also concerned that when the government is making suggestions that export of cryptography or key recovery or whatever must be somehow coupled to a government approved public key infrastructure, that's a serious concern that we all should have.

And, so, in my testimony, I made comments that—I guess there is one other point I want to make. When—I think it was in the fall of 1993—the appropriation was first made for that study that was concluded in 1996, there was a great, "Oh, good. It's going to take them at least 2 years to do that, and we don't have to do anything until they have, in fact, finished their study." And, public key infrastructure is something we need so badly that the notion that let's put it off to a study for—I mean, it's going to take 6 or 8 months for it to get started and then 18 months for it to conclude.

So, to say that we are not going to do anything about moving ahead with the public key infrastructure until after the results of an NRC study are done again, I think is really, at this point—if this study can be expanded to more things of the sort that Marc is talking about, it's probably a very useful thing to do. To say let's focus it on public key infrastructure, these things can actually do harm because they put off—not the results of them but the fact that it's going to take 2 years for them to happen.

And, so that's my concern with focusing on something that we so desperately need, that it may cause a lot of people to decide, "I'm not going to do anything about public key infrastructure until after the results have happened." And, that puts us into the next millennium. And, we just don't need that.

Mr. EHLERS. Any other comments? Dr. Diffie.

Mr. DIFFIE. A public key infrastructure is something whose virtues arise almost entirely out of standardization. And, we have at the moment a standard standardization problem; namely, we need something desperately.

We are inclined to rush forward into it. Many people are inclined and, therefore, come out in competition.

If, by regulation, you select one of the competitors, you risk something like the experience with NTSC in television, which has cursed us in North America now for two generations. But, in return, we have the benefit of having television ahead of other people.

I think there is— once again, there is a research problem of the sort that NIST exists to work on which is, "Can we do something to coordinate efforts in public key infrastructure without, at the same time, tying people's hands, imposing unnecessary restrictions, et cetera?" I don't know the answer to that question.

But, I am not convinced that NRC—that a study is the right action here. It's something much more like a coordinating committee that seems to me to be needed.

And, it just occurs to me, I mean, maybe the Computer Security Advisory Board would be a more appropriate group to be talking to everybody and to act as a forum for coordination among the various public key infrastructure activities that are already underway.

Mr. EHLERS. Mr. Bidzos.

Mr. BIDZOS. Well, I think what has happened is we've got this wall between industry and government, because we have totally different standards. Dr. Diffie is absolutely correct that those 2 years that we waited for the NRC report resulted in rapid development and progress in a public key infrastructure outside of government.

As I mentioned in my earlier comments, we have 100 million products that do inter-operate, that talk to—most of them talk to each other. They are based on standards that not only go to the encryption and the algorithm but formats and these credentials called "certificates," all this sort of stuff. That all works.

And, I think, again, the bill is right on in terms of telling NIST to take a look at what the market is doing and plug into it, plug into that infrastructure; don't try to build your own, because you tried that and that hasn't worked.

And, so the bill addresses that problem, I think, that way.

Now, having somebody who looks at ways to make sure that these are coordinated efforts, that's very important. And, that was sort of my interpretation, making sure.

But, basically if we are correcting legislation that was introduced 10 years ago, it's worth investing a year of somebody's time to make sure that it's working so that we know in 1998 rather than 2008 that we've really gotten what we thought we were going to get from this bill.

Mr. EHLERS. Any other comments? Any other issues that anyone on the panel wishes to raise or any questions that you want to raise?

[No response.]

Mr. EHLERS. If not, I certainly thank you for your time and your attention and, above all, your expertise. It has been a very good panel.

I've learned a lot, and I'm sure the Committee has. We appreciate your comments on the bill and look forward to further contact with you.

Thank you very much. The meeting stands adjourned.

[Whereupon, at 12:50 p.m., Thursday, June 19, 1997, the hearing was adjourned.]

[The following material was received for the record:]

TESTIMONY
THE HOUSE SCIENCE SUB-COMMITTEE
in behalf of the
COMPUTER SYSTEM SECURITY AND PRIVACY ADVISORY BOARD

WILLIS H. WARE, Chairman
June 19, 1997

The Computer System Security and Privacy Advisory Board (CSSPAB) was established
by the Computer Security Act of 1987 [PL 100-235]. The Act specifies the membership
as four each from the Government, from recognized experts in the computer and
telecommunications industry, and from recognized experts "eminent in the [same fields]
but not employed by a producer of equipment." The mission of the Board is "to identify
emerging managerial, technical, administrative and physical safeguard issues relative to
computer system security and privacy, to advise the Bureau of Standards [sic] and the
Secretary of Commerce on such matters, and to report its findings to the Secretary of
Commerce, Director of OMB, Director of NSA, and appropriate committees of
Congress." In discharging its duties, the Board has interpreted its mission broadly,
although to date, it has concentrated on security issues to the exclusion of personal
privacy ones. It usually conveys its findings to relevant recipients in the form of
resolutions adopted in public meetings under the provisions of the Federal Advisory
Committee Act. It occasionally uses the less formal approach of a letter of discussion.

The Board at its March 1997 meeting had decided that, since the Act is now 10 years old,
it should devote a large part of its June 1997 meeting to a reexamination of the Computer
Security Act, and inquire about its effectiveness in improving the information-system
security posture of the civil Federal agencies. To this end, the Board received a series of
presentations from Congresswoman Constance Morella, [retired USAF] General Robert
T. Marsh (chairman of the PCCIP), Mr. Stewart Baker (formerly General Counsel of
NSA), Mr. Bruce McConnell (OIRA/OMB), and representatives of several civil agencies.
Government members of the Board also provided comments reflecting their own
agencies' experience.

The Board heard a generally consistent theme; namely, that the structure and wording of
the Act (as now in place) is satisfactory for the purposes enumerated in it, but the
implementation has had significant shortfalls. The Board does, however, acknowledge
that new obligations and purposes could be added to the Act; but since a specific
legislative proposal (in particular, the proposed Computer Security Enhancement Act of
1997) was not on the table, the Board choose not to make recommendations for statutory
change at this time.

Section 3 of the 1987 Act established a Computer Standards Program under the National
Bureau of Standards (now NIST). It was stipulated to cover "a broad range of technical,
administrative, personnel, and physical security issues." Behind this assigned
responsibility was an implication that an appropriate array of standards, guidelines and

procedures would automatically assure that civil agencies would be able to achieve an adequate information-system security posture. This assumption proved not to be true for various reasons: among them, the civil agencies did not have and could not acquire appropriate expertise, the pace of technology advance far outstripped the ability of the security community to keep up, the motivation for civil agencies to expend funds on information security issues was virtually absent. As would be expected in a competition for funds, the agency mission obligations far outweighed security considerations, and Congress did not provide supplementary funding for security improvements.

While the Act directs NIST to provide technical assistance to civil agencies in implementing standards and guidelines, it does not require NIST to provide general system-level security advice and overall assistance to civil agencies.

Yet, this last is precisely what civil agencies require and consistently said as much to the Board. This is not a new message to the Board; it has heard such pleas for help over the years. Indeed, it was the motivation for the Board many years ago, to persuade NIST to write its well received Computer Security Handbook.

So to speak, the civil agencies need system-level "handholding" in the design of the security safeguards for a system, in the choice of appropriate security products, in assembling security products into an overall system-wide security structure, in the choice of appropriate operational procedures and relevant policies, in rapid response technical support when problems emerge. In short, the civil agencies need the "whole ball of wax" in regard to assistance and support for their info-security obligations.

The NIST management interpreted its mission under the Act differently. While it has cooperated with civil agencies by establishing several Federal Information Processing Standards, and while it did produce a comprehensive Computer Security Handbook (at the urging of the CSSPAB) and other supporting documents, as a general rule NIST has chosen not to involve itself with direct assistance to civil agencies but rather to emphasize various research efforts that would benefit U.S. industry. The issue of information security, particularly for Federal agencies, simply does not appear to have been high on the NIST priority list; but wherever it has been, direct assistance to civil agencies has been even lower. The divergence between the direction of NIST's information security efforts with its industry focus, and the needs of the civil agencies is the sense in which agencies indicate that implementation of the Act has been flawed.

OMB Circular A-130, especially appendix 3, is more direct than the 1987 Act in urging NIST to provide direct assistance to civil agencies, but it has not been successful either in rectifying the divergence just noted.

To address this issue and hopefully encourage NIST to be more responsive in its direct-support activities, the Board adopted two resolutions on June 6, 1997 (copies attached). The first makes two major points:

    a. That NIST elevate its commitment to direct assistance of the civil agencies with regard to information-system security; and

    b. That it do so with stronger managerial focus and allocation of resources to such a commitment.

Resolution 97-1 also includes five detailed actions which the Board regarded as important aspects of a significantly stronger commitment to supporting civil agencies with their information-security problems of today -- the so called "now problem" as opposed to the "tomorrow problem" of future needs which appears to have been NIST's primary focus of activity.

The second, resolution 97-2, addresses one of the five specific points in resolution 97-1 and sets forth some attributes of a registry of security and privacy incidents, together with problems and solutions. The Board felt it essential to single out this one detail for a supplementary resolution because the status of information security in the civil agencies is generally not really known. Their security posture is typically considered to be at the lower margin of satisfactory, primarily on the basis of the number of incidents, events, and penetrations that are reported or otherwise suspected of occurring. But in truth, no one really know what the true situation is.

With the escalating importance of the Information Warfare threat and the increased vigilance that civil agencies will be expected to achieve, the country must have a means to know what its information-security posture is, and whether it is growing stronger in response to technically more sophisticated and persistent threats.

Especially important is the Board's conviction that "to avoid compromise of [Federal civil agency] systems, it is imperative that certain aspects of this [collected] information be protected from disclosure. For example, details about the precise nature of the attack must be protected to prevent it from becoming a "cookbook" for hacker attackers [or becoming pointers to exploitable vulnerabilities.]"

In responding to an increased participation of direct support, NIST has at least three choices for management to follow. The Board takes no position on which is preferred, particularly since the Board is careful not to drift into micro-management of NIST affairs.

NIST could acquire, or develop, the relevant staff skills and create a few teams of broadly based experts to interact with civil agencies needing support; or it could qualify and certify other organizations as having relevant expertise (as it now does in the NVLAP program for certifying special purpose testing laboratories); or it could follow a mixed strategy -- create one or two teams and extend their capability with certified private sector sources. Thus, a civil agency could expect to receive a roster of certified and qualified sources from which it could select and contract, and/or some, perhaps limited, direct support from NIST.

Research managers are quick to point out that productive people in R&D are typically ones who maintain a reasonable interaction and contact with the real world to which they expect to contribute new knowledge. A direct-assistance civil agency support effort would work to NIST's R&D benefit in exactly the same manner. Neither an R&D group or a direct-assistance group is more important than the other; they co-exist synergistically for both which implies, among other things, that the respective personnel must share equally in opportunities for career progression, promotion, salary advancement and other rewards.

Respectfully submitted.

Willis H. Ware
Chairman, CSSPAB

Encl: Resolution 97-1
          Resolution 97-2

COMPUTER SYSTEM SECURITY AND PRIVACY ADVISORY BOARD

Resolution 97-1

June 6, 1997

In order to enhance security and privacy of Federal information, and to strengthen the implementation of the Computer Security Act of 1987, Federal agencies should receive additional computer security guidance and assistance for selection and implementation of computer products, systems, and applications. Increased focus will enhance the economy and efficiency of computer systems security and privacy in the Federal government.

Therefore, we resolve:

That NIST should elevate its commitment to implementing the Computer Security Act of 1987 by increasing its assistance to the civilian Federal agencies. Greater managerial focus and resources should address current computer security and privacy issues, including greater emphasis on today's managerial and administrative aspects. High priority items NIST should address include:

- Act as central service within the Federal government to advise on the selection, integration, and use of products and procedures for securing non-classified systems.

- Provide a computer systems security assessment capability for civilian Federal agencies.

- Maintain a register of security and privacy incidents, problems and solutions (in accordance with Resolution 97-2). Provide suggested corrective actions to remedy computer security vulnerabilities which have been identified.

- Maintain a repository and act as a clearing house for information, techniques, guidelines, and consultation to aid proper use of security features available in government-used commercial off-the-shelf software.

- Identify exemplary activities within Federal agencies that can be used as models and proof-of-concepts for secure civilian government systems.

FOR: Burns, Layton, Leo, Parker, Sanovic, Spix, Vetter, Weingarten
AGAINST: None
ABSTAIN: None
ABSENT: Fisher*

*Present for meeting but not available for this vote

COMPUTER SYSTEM SECURITY AND PRIVACY ADVISORY BOARD

Resolution 97-2

June 6, 1997

In order to enhance security and privacy of Federal information systems and their data, and to strengthen the implementation of the Computer Security Act of 1987, information should be gathered about security events and vulnerabilities which exist in Federal computer systems. Such information provides a basis for security and privacy problems that may exist in multiple locations, be a repository for solutions to such problems, and a source of statistics by which progress for individual sites and for the Federal government as a whole can be tracked. To avoid compromise of systems, it is imperative that certain aspects of this information be protected from disclosure. For example, details about the precise nature of the attack must be protected to prevent it from becoming a "cookbook" for hacker attackers.

Therefore, we resolve:

That NIST should --

> 1) define the data which must be collected by each civilian agency (e.g., virus attacks, network attacks, exploitation of software flaws, compromise of personal information, etc.);

> 2) develop a repository for the compilation of this data; and

> 3) develop a mechanism to report and track progress in these areas for each civilian Federal agency and for the composite of all.

FOR: Burns, Layton, Leo, Parker, Sanovic, Spix, Vetter, Weingarten
AGAINST: None
ABSTAIN: None
ABSENT: Fischer*

*Present at the meeting but not available for this vote

WILLIS H. WARE

Formally educated in engineering, Dr. Ware has long been concerned with
the impact of computers and information technology upon society, and as
early as the mid-1960s began writing and discussing his views on
computers as a growing social force. He thus combines the sensitivities
of a social scientist with the detailed knowledge of a technologist.

In 1946, he became one of the original members of the staff of the
Electronic Computer Project at Princeton's Institute for Advanced Study.
There he worked on the design and development of the large-scale,
general-purpose electronic digital computer. In 1952, Dr. Ware joined
the staff of The RAND Corporation. He served as Head of the Computer
Sciences Department (now the Information Sciences Department) from 1964
to 1971, when he became Deputy Vice President for Project RAND (USAF).
He is presently a member of the Corporate Research Staff. His work has
included the development of large computers and their application to
military, scientific, and industrial problems. His experience spans all
aspects of information systems--hardware, software, system design, and
acquisition management.

In 1967, he organized a series of papers that discussed for the first
time the importance and complexity of computer security, and in 1970
presented a paper proposing specific privacy guidelines. As Chairman of
the DHEW Committee on Automated Personal Data Systems, he presented a
report to Secretary Weinberger and Attorney General Richardson which has
become the definitive document on privacy problems and proposed solutions.

In 1974, he was appointed chairman of a special committee on privacy
by AFIPS, a national professional society. In the same year he presented
talks at privacy conferences in Tokyo, Paris, and Vienna.

In 1975, he was appointed by the White House to the Privacy Protection
Study Commission created by the Privacy Act of 1974. As Vice Chairman,
Dr. Ware spent the next two years with the Commission studying data
banks and information systems, public and private, across the country.
Findings and recommendations were reported to the President and to the
Congress in July 1977.

His efforts on behalf of individual privacy in the age of electronic
information processing earned him DPMA's Computer Sciences Man-of-the-Year
Award in June 1975 and other awards.

He is a Fellow of the Institute of Electrical and Electronics Engineers,
and a member of the National Academy of Engineering and of the American
Association for the Advancement of Science. He is a recipient of the U.S.
Air Force Exceptional Civilian Service Medal and the 1984 IEEE Centennial
Medal. He has chaired or is a member of many governmental advisory
groups.

Additional Questions for the Record
The Honorable Gary Bachula

Question #I:
What, in your opinion, is the significance of the Data Encryption Standard (DES)
being broken as announced on June 19th, 1997? What was NIST's role in
developing the DES? What procedures did NIST follow? What input did NIST
receive?

Answers:

Recent DES "Break" - The method reportedly used to break the DES was a brute
force attack, reportedly involving approximately 78,000 computers working for
four months. This effort required considerable computing power in order to find
one cryptographic key and to decode one message. This does not present a
true threat to the vast majority of information protected by DES. The DES
continues to be safe particularly for those applications with a short security life.
Consistent with existing computer security practices, users are advised to
change cryptographic keys frequently and to protect their keys to minimize risks.
However, users should be aware that their sensitive information could be
compromised if an attacker is willing to put considerable resources into the
effort. New algorithms will be needed to protect highly sensitive data. NIST has
started a public process to develop the Advanced Encryption Standard.

Development of DES - The enclosed paper, "The Data Encryption Standard:
Past and Future" by Miles Smid and Dennis K. Branstad documents the
development of DES and addresses issues regarding the history of DES. This
paper was published in the Proceedings of the IEEE in May, 1988. To
summarize, NIST: 1) made DES the federal standard, 2) developed a DES
conformance testing program, and 3) worked with ANSI to adopt DES as an
ANSI standard.

Question #2:
Section 7, as written, does not impact the export control of encryption products.
Do you believe that by simply quantifying the strength of foreign encryption
products we will harm national security?

Answer: Determinations of the national security implications of quantifying
the strength of foreign encryption products are not NIST's to make. NIST
focuses on establishing techniques for testing security products (including
cryptographic products) conformance to standards and accrediting private
laboratories to perform the tests.

Question #3:

Has NIST, in the past, established computer security standards that industry did not support? Did such standards achieve the results NIST desired? What, in your opinion, went wrong with the Clipper initiative?

Answer: NIST's primary responsibility is to ensure that the U.S. economy has the measurement capability and standards needed for trade and industry. In addition, NIST has a particular responsibility to assist government in carrying out its mission(s) by establishing needed measurements and standards. By working with voluntary standards system, NIST generally is able to meet both of those needs. However, in some cases, NIST must work within the government when it has specific needs that are not being met by the normal process.

Two security standards, in particular, were designed to meet government needs and did not require the widespread industry support that we usually seek and obtain, such as in the success of DES. To meet its responsibility to assist other agencies, NIST sometimes works with them to establish standards to meet specific government needs. In the computer area, in particular, NIST has a responsibility to promulgate federal information processing standards in those areas where a particular government need is not being met by industrial standards. We do not expect that solutions that meet the needs of one or more government agencies will always be widely adopted by industry. The "clipper" initiative occurred in the context of a lack of private sector responses to particular governmental needs. What has changed since that time is the emergence of services and products in the private sector that did not exist at that time.

Question #4:

When NIST developed the Digital Signature Standard did they make full use of available commercial standards? In retrospect, and given the fact that Federal agencies are now turning to commercially available products, would it have been more useful for NIST to adopt a commercially available standard at the outset?

Answer: The Digital Signature Standard is a Federal Information Processing Standard for use by the Federal government. NIST did consider commercially available products during the initial considerations, but the needs of some Federal agencies made the commercial products inappropriate. As those agencies, requirements evolve, it is likely to become possible to encourage wider appropriate use of commercially available products. Please note that the Department has sought public comment on additional digital signature technologies and algorithms that would be appropriate for government use.

Question #5:
Do you agree that more money dedicated to fellowships and grants to support students studying computer security will help to improve the nation's security?

Answer: Yes, and we strongly support your efforts to provide for computer security fellowships in institutions of higher learning.

Responses to Questions for the Record by the Hon. Bart Gordon, Ranking Member, Subcommittee on Technology, Committee on Science, U.S. House of Representatives

Hearing on the Computer Security Enhancement Act of 1997

Question 1:
At its June 6 meeting, your department's outside advisory committee, the Computer System Security and Privacy Advisory Board, passed resolutions that call on NIST to exert greater efforts in carrying out its responsibilities under the Computer Security Act of 1987 for protecting non-classified electronic information in Federal computer systems.

- Would you agree that the recommendations of the Advisory Board are consistent with provisions in the legislation regarding, for example, federal response to security incidents and assisting agencies in the selection of commercial off-the-shelf security products?

Answer: In passing its Resolutions, the Board noted that such activities are consistent with current authorities and responsibilities assigned to NIST in the Computer Security Act of 1987.

- What actions will NIST take in response to the Advisory Board's recommendations?

Answer: NIST will be carefully considering the Board's recommendations for improving direct support to agencies as they develop program plans in this critical area. We have not yet determined the specific actions that we will take.

Question 2:
How should NIST improve its efforts to carry out its responsibilities under the Computer Security Act, and do you have specific examples of steps the agency could take to do so?

Answer: NIST currently has a number of programs in place to meet its Computer Security Act responsibilities. The Federal Computer Incident Response Capability (FedCIRC) activity, which we have already discussed in detail with the committee, is but one example of such a program. Given the current demands on NIST, available resources, and NIST's responsibilities to assist both the public and private sectors, additional program activities cannot be initiated without harming important programs that are underway.

- What is your view of the Advisory Board's recommendation for NIST to provide more direct consultation and support to agencies on computer security matters?

Answer: Most of the direct agency assistance services are readily available from the private sector. Thus, when such consultative expertise exists in the private sector, it is usually unnecessary and generally inappropriate for NIST to offer such services. However, NIST does, from time to time, accept such work from other agencies, usually on a reimbursable basis and when NIST has unique skills to offer in an advanced technology area or when the particular area is consistent with NIST's research agenda. In this way, NIST's computer security agency assistance activities benefit both NIST and the particular agency -- and this usually results in guidance that can benefit all agencies with similar needs.

-Are the resources currently allocated by NIST adequate to meet the goals of the Computer Security Act?

Answer: We believe that the current level of effort devoted to the computer security program at NIST is adequate for today's activities. However, if NIST is going to be expected to take on new efforts to protect the nation's critical infrastructures or support electronic commerce, the resource issue will have to be re-addressed.

Question 3:
Has the Department of Commerce taken any initiative to inform the public of the vulnerabilities of computers and networks and of the value of the use of encryption technologies? For example, NIST recently sponsored an international conference on the Year 2000 computer problem. What do you believe is the Department's role in providing information to the public on security threats in the world of electronic commerce?

Answer: In short, NIST has, indeed, taken several initiatives to inform the public (i.e., users and managers of computers and networks) of both the vulnerabilities and protective measures, including encryption. Through its Computer Security Resource Clearinghouse (http://csrc.nist.gov) NIST has for several years made available threat information in the form of alerts and pointers to other resources and sites containing detailed information. Moreover, the NIST-managed Federal Computer Incident Response Capability (FedCIRC) makes available such information via its web site at http://fedcirc.llnl.gov/.

In FY 97 alone, NIST has produced and conducted four tutorials/workshops on Internet security and incident handling. We plan four more by October. We have briefed, since last October, more than a dozen agencies on FedCIRC, responded to 143 inquiries, responded to 131 government sites, distributed twenty security advisories, and welcomed over 17,000 visitors to our FedCIRC web site. Additionally, the Computer Security Institute, under NIST auspices, held six workshops and training sessions, on a variety of computer security topics. Finally, we have produced almost a dozen security bulletins in FY 96/97.

NIST also addresses threats and vulnerabilities of computer systems in its computer security guidance publications; see for example Chapter 4, "Common Threats: A Brief Overview," in *NIST's An Introduction to Computer Security: The NIST Handbook* (available at http://csrc.nist.gov/nistpubs/800-12/). NIST also publishes bulletins on computer security threats and related issues (See, for example, http://csrc.nist.gov/nistbul/csl94-03.txt.) NIST has, of course, also developed a standard and accompanying conformance tests for the security of cryptographic modules.

Clearly, we believe in the importance of making users aware of the threats to and vulnerabilities of computer systems. However, it must also be understood that encryption is just a part of the solution; it is not a cure-all. Systems must be protected with an appropriate combination of administrative, technical, and managerial controls. Technical solutions, including encryption, will be ineffective and will provide a false sense of security if they are not implemented and managed properly.

Question 4:
Two central elements of the draft version of the White House's upcoming policy statement on electronic commerce call for the government to follow industry's lead and to do everything possible to encourage widespread use of electronic commerce. Are the provisions of H.R. 1903 consistent with those goals? -If not, why shouldn't NIST be given more responsibility in encouraging the civilian use of encryption technologies?

Answer: As indicated at the hearing, there are a number of elements in the bill to which the Administration does not object. We look forward to working with the Committee, based on our testimony at the hearing, to address those concerns that were expressed. With regard to "encouraging the civilian use of encryption technologies", as noted above, encryption is not a cure all for looking at systematic issues of vulnerability.

Question 5:
Would you explain in more detail your objections to section 7 of the bill? -In the current encryption debate, why wouldn't we want a "neutral" source to validate industry claims that stronger encryption products are easily available abroad? These provisions don't impact the Administration's currently licensing procedure - they simply provide additional information on which to base decisions.

Answer: As indicated at the hearing, the Administration stated a number of concerns about this provision. First, the activities proposed for NIST in section 7 would not "provide additional information on which to base decisions." Market availability based on encryption strength is not a factor in licensing decisions. Second, the inclusion of these essentially regulatory provisions clouds the bill's stated objective of improving the security of Federal Government systems. The proposed section would inappropriately put NIST, a non-regulatory agency, in the position of second guessing both existing regulatory processes and existing executive branch determinations.

Question 6:
Dr. Ware, Chairman of the Computer System Security and Privacy Advisory Board (CSSPAB), submitted testimony to the Subcommittee stating, "The Board heard a generally consistent theme; namely, that the structure and working of the Act (as now in place) is satisfactory for the purposes enumerated in it, but implementation has had significant shortfalls. The Board does acknowledge that new obligations and purposes could be added to the Act; ..." Mr. Bachula what has contributed to the implementation shortfalls at NIST and how would you recommend that they be corrected? Also do you intend to solicit the Board's views on whether the Computer Security Act of 1987 needs to be updated?

Answer: The "shortfall" described by the Board was in the area of direct agency assistance, as addressed in Question 2 above. In FY 96/97 direct agency reimbursable support was provided to a diverse group of agencies, such as Treasury, Agriculture, Library of Congress, Panama Canal Commission, Federal Aviation Administration, and the Environmental Protection Agency on subjects ranging from Internet connectivity to vulnerability analysis to security certification and accreditation.

Regarding the Board's views on updating the Computer Security Act, the Board, at its June meeting, examined the Act and just that question. We have made Board minutes, reports, and recommendations available to the committee.

5

Responses to

Computer Security Enhancement Act of 1997
Additional Questions for the Record

Dr. Whitfield Diffie
Distinguished Engineer

Sun Microsystems
Palo Alto, California

Q)Can you explain for us from your vantage point the importance of NIST's continued role in the setting of standards in computer security for Federal civilian agencies?

What advantages do you see in keeping the responsibility for setting computer security standards for Federal civilian agencies with NIST?

A)What is important is to recognize that information security (computer security and communication security --- in particular, cryptography) is now main stream commercial and industrial technology, not specialized military technology. Standards for information security should therefore be set through an open process by agencies that are part of the main stream federal standards process, not by secretive organizations that only became involved because at one time they had the only available expertise. There may be other civilian agencies to which this responsibility could be assigned, but NIST seems as plausible a choice as any.

Q)What do you believe would be the result of a Federal policy that divests NIST of its jurisdiction and give these duties to National Security Agency?

A)A complete subjection of civilian security to NSA's intelligence agenda and continuing delay in securing the US information infrastructure.

Q)Can you describe for us what benefit you believe is derived from private sector and industry involvement in the process of establishing computer security standards for Federal agencies?

A)The current trend in government procurement in all areas is to make use of commercial standards and products wherever possible. This decline in the use of exclusively or primarily federal products reduces the need for distinct federal standards. An appropriate role of federal standards organizations is now to participate in private sector standardization efforts as both expert contributor and representative of a large customer.

Q)Can you comment on the announcement of the breaking of the Data Encryption Standard (DES) on June 19th, 1997 and its significance to the setting of standards for computer security?

A)The demonstration that DES could be broken by a coalition of enthusiasts using readily available computers shows that DES is no longer adequate to protect some of the information for which it is currently used. It also suggests that the decision to limit the strength of DES when it was adopted twenty years ago was shortsighted.

DES must be replaced and awareness of the mistakes made in the adoption of DES should guide that replacement. The cost of replacing existing DES based equipment and protocols will only be painful. Given the rate at which secure communication is growing, if the successor to DES requires replacement in twenty to twenty-five years, the costs will be crippling.

Q)Do you think that additional moneys for computer security fellowships and grants will help to improve the nation's security?

A)Yes. We have the opportunity to train a new generation of security specialists who have grown up amid computer and will therefore have an instinctive understanding of society's need for security in the digital age.

Q)Has NIST, in the past, established computer security standards that industry did not support?

A)Yes. FIPS 185 (key escrow) and FIPS 186 (digital signature) are examples of this.

Q)Did such standards achieve the results NIST desired?

A)It is hard to know what NIST desired. Neither of the standards cited above achieved the results that are usually described as a successful standard.

Q)What was wrong with the Clipper initiative?

A)It completely ignored reality and reflected only NSA's desire not to have cryptosystems whose traffic it could not readily read outside of its control.

A cryptographic system for widespread use in civilian government must represent a private sector sector standard both to reduce costs and to promote secure communication between the government and the rest of society. A cryptographic system that is to be a widespread commercial standard must be transnational because the US is only 5% of the world's population and more than half of the business of the major US companies is with foreign customers. Such a system must also be amenable to software implementation or it will be used in only a small fraction of the possible applications.

Clipper ignored all of these factors. Its algorithm was secret, which made it unpalatable and inaccessible to foreigners. Its implementation was restricted to hardware which made it expensive. Its escrow provisions were unacceptable to most potential customers in the US and virtually all customers outside the US.

Q)When NIST developed the Digital Signature Standard did they make full use of available commercial standards?

A)No.

Q)In retrospect, and given the fact that Federal agencies are now turning to commercially available products would it have been more useful for NIST to adopt a commercially available standard at the outset?

A)Yes.

Responses to
Questions Submitted for the Record
by the
Hon. Bart Gordon (D-TN)
Ranking Member
Subcommittee on Technology
Committee on Science

Hearing on the Computer Security Enhancement Act of 1997
19 June 1997

Dr. Whitfield Diffie
Distinguished Engineer

Sun Microsystems
Palo Alto, California

1a. I believe that federal efforts to promote ``greater use of cryptography''
would be helpful. I believe that all that is necessary is an end to
federal interference with the deployment of cryptography.

1b. The are several areas in which the Department of Commerce can make
valuable contributions to the use of cryptography as an enabling
technology for electronic commerce and an ``information democracy.''

Under regulations that went into effect on 1 January 1997, the DoC has
been given greater authority and responsibility for regulating the
export of cryptography but appears, in the process, to have imported
both Department of State personnel and policies. Instructions from the
Secretary to the effect that exports should be permitted, wherever
possible, would would be very helpful. In particular, the foreign
availability test should govern and cryptographic products should
always be exportable when equivalent products are available abroad.

In the area of information security standards, the direction of the
recent NIST efforts to develop an Advanced Encryption Standard are
commendable and represent a desirable change from the style of security
standards development pursued in recent years. Every effort should be
made to support this change of direction and to guarantee that NIST
has adequate resources to continue on its present course.

1c. A central, public, clearinghouse on information security threats would
be a valuable contribution on NIST's part. Communications interception
and network penetration are especially valuable tools of criminals and
spies because they are very hard to detect. Confidential information
that has been ``stolen'' does not disappear like stolen physical
property. The the fact that corporate plans or designs have become
known to competitors may only become visible in the form of business
losses. Even when intrusion is suspected, it is often difficult to
trace. These inherent problems in combating threats to information
security are complicated by a wall of silence surrounding penetrations
of corporate communications. Corporations are not required to report
such penetrations even when they detect them and have found that to do
so threatens customer confidence.

The prestige and investigative abilities of a federal agency could play
a major role in breaking down the wall of silence and giving the
business community a solid base of information on which to base its
information security activities.

2. The single most valuable step the government could take to promote the
development of a national infrastructure to support commercial and
private uses of encryption technologies would be to relax export
controls on cryptographic software embedded in operating systems and
applications and endorse the legitimacy of commercial and private use
of encryption. If this is done, the major hardware and software
manufacturers will expand their information security efforts several
substantially and a national information security infrastructure will
develop rapidly.

Some government representatives have suggested that freer export of
cryptographic products from the United States would be met with trade
barriers against such products abroad. To the extent that this occurs,
the Department of Commerce should support US industry by opposing such
foreign action in the same way the US government opposes other trade
barriers.

Development of standards that reflect the multinational commercial needs
for encryption and the true costs of information security could speed
the development of the information security infrastructure.

3. Any governmental action with respect to digital signatures should be
limited to areas where new law or regulation is actually necessary and

purely commercial actions base on law of contract appear unlikely to succeed. Insofar as possible, new ``legislation'' should be limited to the digital signature process itself and should not intrude on existing commercial law with respect to signatures or associated credentials.

Because digital signatures, unlike handwritten signatures, are not a property of the individual, a legal definition of when a digital process will be considered the digital signature of an individual would be helpful. This should include provisions to guarantee that an individual can never be held responsible for a digital signature if any other entity was in possession the information needed to create the signature.

4. The decisions we make about issues of information security cannot be value neutral. They will increase the power of some groups and decrease the power of others. Consensus is not likely to be reached in under a generation. This said, an open forum with access to expertise and information may play a constructive role in reaching positions that reflect the broad interests of society rather than merely those groups affected first.

5. NIST's shortcomings in carrying out the purposes of the Computer Security act of 1987 can be traced to its dependence on NSA, an organization that devotes the major portion of its budget to intelligence activities rather than security. In order to function independently and in the service of American industry, NIST's information security activities must be better supported and freed of any requirement for NSA concurrence.

In particular, any ``Interagency Working Group'' or other mechanism to guarantee NSA a secret preview and a an effective veto on NIST plans is incompatible with the intentions of the Act.

6. Effective collaboration between NIST and NSA under the present legal and funding framework appears impossible. The escrowed encryption standard (FIPS 186) illustrates the problems. Although FIPS 186 is a Department of Commerce standard, it relies on secret technology that is ``owned'' by an agency of the Department of Defense. Such an arrangement undermines the integrity and independence of the DoC. It cannot, for example, guarantee that its standard remains in force, because NSA controls access to the technology by contractors who produce the chips implementing the standard.

Only a regime in which the Secretary of Commerce was given original top
secret classification authority and the Department of Defense was
instructed to provide classified technology in accord with DoC's view
of its needs (and in which DoC had broad power to declassify
appropriate portions of the technology) would allow satisfactory
collaboration. This seems unlikely.

The best we can hope for is that NIST can be mandated to function
independently of NSA and can adequately serve the needs of American
society on this basis.

7. Evaluating commercially available information security products to the
degree required for a ``seal of approval'' might be prohibitively
expensive. A worthwhile and less costly approach would be to publish
functional descriptions of commercially available products and
coordinating the analytic efforts of academic and industrial
researchers in studying the systems. This would be similar in style to
the AES development.

8. I believe that NIST's failure to engage the energy and productivity of
the US computer and communications industries has been an outgrowth of
its unresponsiveness to industry's needs and its subordination to NSA's
desires. It is too early to say whether the development of an Advanced
Encryption Standard is a genuine departure from this pattern, but all
signs so far are that it is. NIST should be encouraged to pursue its
new open approach on all fronts.

The impact of NIST's failure to develop appropriate security standards
during the 1980s has probably been to delay the introduction of proper
security into American computer and communication systems by a decade.
Had NIST gone on to develop a standard for public key cryptography at
the time is solicited for one in 1982, the country might now be far
safer from ``information warfare'' attacks on its critical
infrastructure.

Hearing on the "Computer Security Enhancement Act of 1997"
June 19, 1997

<u>**Responses to Questions for the Record**</u>

Stephen T. Walker
President and CEO, Trusted Information Systems, Inc. (TIS)

Dear Madame Chairwoman:

Thank you for having invited me to testify at your June 19, 1997 hearing on H.R. 1903, the Computer Security Enhancement Act of 1997, and for giving me the opportunity to express my views on enhancing computer security and the role of the Computer System Security and Privacy Board.

As my written and oral testimony indicated, I support H.R. 1903 and strongly support the provisions that will accomplish the objectives of strengthening- NIST's mission and capabilities for providing computer system security guidance and assistance to federal agencies and that will enhance the role and resources of the Board. My responses to the additional questions you have posed for the record are provided below.

1.   Do you think that the Computer System Security and Privacy Advisory Board is still needed and useful? Might other information security-related boards be able to replace or supersede its functions?

The Board is most certainly still needed and still useful! Over the past decade, the Board has provided public visibility into the processes by which federal cryptographic and information security policies have been developed and implemented. As information technologies continue to increase in social and economic importance, the need for public visibility, participation, and confidence in the processes and means by which our information systems are being safeguarded also increases. I am not aware of other existing or proposed boards that could individually or in concert provide the same degree of openness and public participation.

2.   In your testimony you indicate it would be desirable for the Computer System Security and Privacy Board ("Board") to be able provide the Secretary of Commerce with recommendations on proposed security standards before they are promulgated. Could you give examples, based on your experiences, of instances when such Board recommendations would have been useful?

As I noted during my oral testimony, the Board may not wish to, or may not be able to, address each and every computer security standard (i.e., Federal Information Processing

Standard, or FIPS) or Guideline that is developed. However, Board consideration of (selected) standards and 0
Guidelines and Board recommendations to the Secretary of Commerce regarding those will increase openness and public participation. Such a mechanism would have been both appropriate and useful during the promulgation of the Digital Signature Standard and the Escrowed Encryption Standard. It is noteworthy that Board meetings and special hearings during 1993 assembled the only public record of government activities during the escrowed-encryption initiative. Board recommendations regarding forthcoming FIPS such as the Advanced Encryption Standard would be useful for focusing public input and for fostering public confidence in of the standard once promulgated.

3.   In your testimony you state that you strongly support an enhanced NIST role in providing practical computer system security assistance to federal agencies. Can you expand on this, in terms of why it is needed, and give examples of what kinds of assistance NIST could provide?

It is important that practical assistance to federal agencies be moved to the forefront of the NIST computer security mission, so that NIST can help agencies do the best job possible in protecting their computer systems and that agencies can benefit from a shared knowledge base and pooled resources. Examples of practical assistance would include helping agencies develop (and maintain) technology -neutral information security policies as a foundation for their security
practices, promoting inter-agency information sharing regarding security incidents and vulnerabilities, coordinating federal emergency-response activities, and providing guidance and assistance to agencies as they seek to securely interconnect formerly separate systems and networks.

4.   Do you think that additional moneys for computer security fellowships and grants will help to improve the nation's security?

Good information security can enhance personal privacy, as well as economic security and national security. Fellowships and grants can attract new students, as well as those considering whether to return for additional education, to the field.

<u>Responses to Additional Questions for the Record</u>

1. *The National Academy of Sciences report released last year, entitled Cryptography's Role in Securing the Information Society, suggested that far more government attention ought to be focused on promoting the use of cryptography, particularly in no-confidentiality applications, such as user authentication and integrity checks.*

- *Do you agree with the National Academy's conclusion [in the CRISIS report] on the need for federal efforts to promote the greater use of cryptography?*

Yes, with a focus on "facilitation" rather than on technology development or premature regulation.

- *How should the Department of Commerce serve as an advocate for the greater use of encryption technologies in order to underpin the development of electronic commerce?*

NIST could provide federal agencies with practical guidance on how to apply commercial encryption products in agency applications and provide pilot demonstration projects.

- *Should NIST, for example, provide a central clearinghouse for public information on information security threats?*

This would be a useful function.

2. *What kinds of initiatives could the government take to promote the development of a national infrastructure to support commercial and private uses of encryption technologies?*

and

3. *Is there a Federal role concerning the development of uniform standards and procedures for certification authorities for digital signature? Some states have begun to establish a legal framework for a digital signature infrastructure; what, if any, should be the federal role to encourage the development of consistent requirements?*

Given current proposals by the Administration and some in Congress to link key recovery systems with some form of government-approved key management infrastructure, I think that the most significant thing the federal government can do to promote development and use of encryption technologies and electronic commerce is NOT to force linkages between key recovery and issuance of public-key certificates by "Government-approved" certification authorities. A forced combination would be ill-advised and create unnecessary complications and delays for users. Cryptographic technologies are fast moving, and markets for these are still quite new—and fragile. Electronic commerce is still in the fledgling stage. The marketplace can be expected to make great progress in terms of performance, price, and interoperability over the next few years. This is not the time to crystallize that progress about a particular government view of the future, and that is just what a joint key recovery/certification authority regulatory scheme would do. It would stifle innovation and variety at a most inopportune time.

4. *The bill proposes to expand the role of the Computer System Security and Privacy Board to be a forum for identifying and seeking consensus on computer security, privacy, and cryptography issues of public concern. Is this a workable approach for improving the communications between the government and the interested public and for arriving at consensus positions for these kinds of things?*

The Computer System Security and Privacy Board (CSSPAB) has consistently provided an open forum (sometimes, the <u>only</u> such forum) for public visibility and input into federal cryptography and information security policies and programs. It is indeed a "workable approach." Moreover, provisions in H.R. 1903 that would provide increased financial resources and enhanced Board authorities will enable the Board to address important issues related to computer security, privacy, and cryptography in a more proactive and extensive fashion that has been possible with relatively limited resources to date.

5. *What are the principal reasons in your view for NIST's shortcomings in carrying out the purposes of the Computer Security Act of 1987?*
and
6. *The criticism has been made that the National Security Agency has assumed a more influential role in the implementation of the Computer Security Act than was anticipated by the legislation. What are your views on the nature and extent of the collaboration that should exist between NIST and NSA?*

Insufficient top management priority and insufficient resources for NIST's activities pursuant to its mandated responsibilities under the Computer Security Act fostered public and congressional concerns over implementation of the Act. For a detailed examination of the intent and implementation of the Act, I refer you to some studies done for the Congress by the former Office of Technology Assessment that are available at <http://www.wws.princeton.edu:80/~ota/>. Both *Information Security and Privacy in Network Environments* (1994) and the *Issue Update* (1995) on the same topic examined the relative roles and resources of NIST and NSA in this regard and recommended measures to better fulfill the purposes of the Computer Security Act. I note that the provisions of H.R. 1903 that would: (i) enhance NIST's computer system security capabilities and resources; (ii) move practical assistance to federal agencies into the forefront of the NIST computer security mission; and (iii) enhance the role and resources of the Computer System Security and Privacy Board should serve both to enhance computer security and improve implementation of the Computer Security Act.

7. *The bill tasks NIST to evaluate commercially available security products in order to assist agencies in selection of the most appropriate solutions to protection of their computer systems. . . .Would the panelists care to expand on their views on this point, since knowledge of the capabilities of commercial products would seem to be directly connected to promotion of their use?*

Experience has shown that security product testing and evaluation, particularly qualitative testing and evaluation, is difficult, contentious, and expensive. As I stated in my oral testimony, government efforts to do product evaluations (by the Defense Department) in the 1980s and early 90s were expensive, time consuming, and unsuccessful. Thus, I am concerned that efforts such as those contemplated in Section 4 of H.R. 1903 will not make the best use of NIST's computer security resources and capabilities and will shortchange other activities that would show a better return to agencies and the public. Instead of NIST doing testing and evaluation to determine suitability of commercial products for federal agency use, I believe it is preferable for NIST to accredit private-sector laboratories to test and evaluate commercial products.

8. *All of you indicate that NIST did not sufficiently involve the energy and productivity of the US computer and communications industries in the area of cryptography. What were the causes of this deficiency and how should it be remedied. Also, what do you believe has been the impact of this shortcoming of NIST?*

The lack of openness and public involvement in the process by which the federal government's cryptography policies were developed during the early 1990's necessarily resulted in under-involvement of US industry. Thus, I do not consider that the primary factor was a "shortcoming of NIST" *per se*, but rather a top-down lack of openness on the part of the Executive Branch. Fortunately, things appear to be changing in the right direction with respect to new encryption standards development, because public visibility and input are critical factors for success. In contrast to the closed process by which the "Clipper chip" standard was developed, NIST is including a mechanism for public comment and other inputs at the beginning of the FIPS development process for the Advanced Encryption Standard.

Responses from Mr. James Bidzos
President and CEO
RSA Data Security

Responses to the Questions Posed by the House Technology Subcom-Part 1

>--Can you give us some more information about the successful attack on DES
>that was announced on June 19th, 1997? How does this relate to H.R. 1903?
>
>Answer: The recent successful exhaustion attack on the Data Encryption
>Algorithm was part of a larger cryptographic challenge announced by RSA
>Data Security in January of 1997. We posted messages that had been
>encrypted with different length keys, ranging from 40 to 128 bits, and
>challenged the cryptographic community to mount exhaustion attacks upon
>these messages in order to find the decryption key and obtain access to the
>plain text of the message. Prior to the cracking of the DES encrypted
>message, the 40 and 48 bit challenges were solved. The full details of
>the successful attack on DES are set forth in the attached press release
>and fact sheet issued shortly after the successful decryption of the DES
>message.

I believe the real significance of DES being broken is that NIST is just
now beginning a multi-year effort to replace DES!

>--In your testimony you referred to the Public Key Management
>Infrastructure that is being established through the use of RSA enabled
>products. Can you provide us with additional information that expands upon
>this concept?
>
Answer: The public-key infrastructure should put the capability to make
and verify digital signatures, and to perform public-key encryption, in
the hands of the populace, embedded in widely used applications. It
should be interoperable. Tools and policies for issuing and managing
certificates should be readily available. Broad industry support for the
PKI should exist.

With RSA embedded in 100 million products - every browser, operating
systems, applications, etc., and companies such as Verisign, Netscape,
Microsoft, IBM, and Oracle (and many more) offering CA products and
services, I think it is fair to say the PKI exists.

A good example is as follows: If the federal government was able to
employ this PKI (which it cannot do only because of NIST policy), the
SSA, IRS, and other agencies could simply buy an off-the-shelf CA server
from any of over a dozen companies, and issue certificates to taxpayers
and citizens. Using those certificates in browsers, citizens could

securely access government services such as SSA account review, tax
>return filing, etc. It's all possible right now.
>
>--What is your perspective on the role that NIST has played in the
>development of cryptographic standards over the past ten years? What
>should NIST's role have been?

>Answer: NIST has not acted independently in the area of cryptography over the
>past ten years. The result has been that the NIST and the Federal
>Information Standards process have been used as a means of proliferating
>cryptogrphic solution developed in secret by the National Security Agency.
>These solutions have been intended to optimize the interests of a foreign
>intelligence agency.   The Digital Signature and the Key Escrow Encryption
>(commonly referred to as "Clipper") standards are the products of this ten
>years of effort in the field of commercial cryptography on the part of NIST.
>Neither of these have
>achieved any significant degree of acceptance in the commercial world. It
>is also regretful that the interests of NIST's principal customers, the
>civil agencies of the government have been neglected during this period of
>time.

>NIST and the Department of Commerce should have acted as an
>aggressive advocates for the cryptographic interests of the private sector
>and the civil agencies. In this capacity NIST should have attempted to
>fully understand the nature of the cryptographic marketplace and use market
>driven standards as basis for federal standards. Clearly the standards
>process was used as an attempt to influence the market, rather than to
>conform to it.
>
>--How will allowing for industry input in the standards setting process
>enhance the security of Federal civilian agency systems?
>
>Answer: This question implies that the input of industry is seriously
>considered at the time that policy and standards decisions are made by
>responsible officials. While industry has always had the opportunity to
>comment on the federal standards proposed for adoption, their input has
>been generally disregarded with respect to cryptographic standards over the
>past ten years. For example the Clipper standard received 320 negative
>comments, versus 2 in favor of the adoption of the standard, and it was
>still adopted as a standard.
>
>If there is meaningful response to the input received from industry by NIST
>and other decision makers, the security federal information systems will
>improve due to the ability of government agencies to take advantage of the
>full range of security solutions delivered by the vendor community. This

>has been one of the very unfortunate results of the government's
>cryptography policy over the past few years. Agencies that wanted to use
>commercial products that included a full suite of embedded RSA cryptography
>were discouraged from using the security features of products developed by
>such vendors as Lotus, Netscape, Microsoft, Oracle and many other highly
>regarded vendors. In an environment where industry input in the standards
>process is sincerely solicited and acted upon, federal agencies will be
>able to fully employ market driven cryptography that is fully integrated
>into the most popular commercial products used by agencies and their
>private sector trading partners. It will also create an environment where
>agencies are free to use cryptography, rather that one which has existed
>where agencies have decided not to use "non-standard" cryptography in order
to avoid potential political problems. In short, the government could
>"plug into" the PKI that already exists.
>
>Why is industry acceptance of standards necessary for implementing
>security?
>
>Answer: The government has demonstrated over the past ten years that
>"industry acceptance" is not necessary for implementing security. However
>the events over this period of time have also demonstrated that industry
>acceptance of standards is a critical factor for federal agencies to
>achieve cost effective security. Without industry support, security
>related standards will not be incorporated into the commercial information
>technology products used by government agencies.
>
>Please detail for the Subcommittee our company's experiences in the setting
>of Federal standards in the past? Please detail how the process could be
>improved to benefit computer security at civilian Federal agencies?
>
>Answer: Our primary involvement with the NIST standard setting process
>has been with respect to the Digital Signature Standard. When NIST
>announced in 1989 that they would initiate work on a Digital Signature
>Standard (DSS) we very encouraged about the prospect of having the
>government adopt the RSA algorithm as the basis for the federal standard.
>We believed that the RSA algorithm offered several advantages to the
>government: (1) During the four year period that NIST and NSA labored to
>produce the DSS, the RSA algorithm gained considerable acceptance within
>the private sector as a de facto standard, and (2) The government enjoyed
>license free/royalty free use RSA enabled products by virtue of government
>sponsorship of the research that led to the development of the RSA
>algorithm.
>
>However the government chose to spend considerable sums of public funds to
>develop a new signature algorithm. Throughout the entire process it became

> clear that the government's fundamental objective was to develop a
>competing signature algorithm, which it hoped would displace RSA as the
>commercial standard. This whole effort was justified as serving vague
>national security and public safety objectives. The result of this
>government attempt to intervene in the market has been to isolate the
government from the dynamic product developments made by the US
>information technology community with respect to the application of RSA
>digital signature technology. It is no accident that forty of the
>forty-five
>digital signature prototype projects sponsored by Government Information
>Technology Services Board will utilize the RSA algorithm as the underlying
>signature technology.
>
>I am encouraged by recent developments in government encryption policy.
>NIST has published a Federal Register announcement asking for comment on
>the desirability of expanding the scope of the existing Digital Signature
>Standard to include the RSA algorithm. I would also like to note that the
>recently issued Request for Proposal for the Defense Travel Systems also
>allows the use of RSA enabled products.

>--Can you explain for us from your vantage point the importance of NIST's
>continued role in the setting of standards in computer security for Federal
>civilian agencies?
>
>Answer: I believe that the civil agencies of the government want an
>independent, highly qualified entity to be a center of cryptographic
>excellence that will support their requirements for effective cryptography
>needed for electronic commerce and business process reengineering. They
want and need an organization that understands the dynamics of
>developments in the private sector and will honestly promote their interests
>in the commercial market place. The civil agencies are not interested in
>being
>represented by an entity that is involved in seeking to retard the domestic
>use of cryptography through its involvement in the export control program
>or in using the federal market as a vehicle for increasing demand for
>products, such as Fortezza, developed for the Department of Defense.
>
>However I believe that NIST, perhaps with the assistance of the Congress,
>must reexamine its role and recognize that the interests of its customers,
>the civil agencies, are best served by the adoption of market driven
>cryptographic standards. NIST's real value may be in assisting federal
>agencies apply the power encryption technology provided by the private
>sector to government business applications.
>
>--Do you think that additional moneys for computer security fellowships and

>grants will improve the nation's security?
>
>Answer: Clearly, additional emphasis on computer security as a field of
>serious academic endeavor is required. The fellowship and grants specified
in the Computer Security Enhancement Act appear to be a promising
>technique for stimulating this subject among the academic community.
>
>--How will the Computer Security Enhancement Act of 1997 improve national
>security and help law enforcement?
>
>Answer: I would refer the Committee to one of the most important
>conclusions of the National Research Council study of encryption policy.
>This group of imminent Americans concluded that "...the advantages of more
>widespread use of cryptography outweigh the disadvantages." The study
>panel recognized that cryptography is an under utilized tool that can
>effectively reduces the potential for crime, state sponsored industrial
>espionage and other adverse effects upon national security and public
>safety.
>
The Computer Security Enhancement Act, which seeks to promote the
>effective use of cryptography by government agencies, is consistent with the
>conclusions of the National Research Council report. Federal agencies are
>incurring significant security exposures by not effectively employing
>cryptographic countermeasures for transmitted and stored data. The
>government's interests, and ultimately those of the taxpayers will be best
>served by a policy that promotes the use of cryptography by federal
>agencies.
>
>--What do you believe would be the result of a Federal policy that divests
>NIST's of its jurisdiction over computer security at Federal civilian
>agencies and give these duties to the National Security Agency?
>
>Answer: Such a policy change would be a significant mistake as it would
>place an element of the defense and intelligence communities in charge of
>information systems security for the entire federal government. The
>fundamental principle underlying the Computer security Act of 1987; namely
>that a civil agency should provide leadership for the federal unclassified
>community, remains as valid today as it was ten years. While NIST's
>performance over the past decade has been disappointing to many of us in
>the private sector, I believe that the majority of information technology
securities companies prefer to see NIST in the civil agency leadership
>role, as opposed to NSA.
>
>This is not to denigrate the capabilities or accomplishments of NSA, but
>rather it recognizes that an agency such as NSA has an inherent conflict of

>interest in the field of information systems security. It has been
>demonstrated repeatedly that their intelligence mission takes priority over
>their security mission. The private sector and the civil agencies need a
>champion within that understands the cost constraints that effect security
>related decisions in a business environment. Producing cost effective
>solutions applicable to the unclassified and commercial communities has
>never been one of NSA's strongest accomplishments.
>
>The net result of such a policy would be further estrangement of the public
>and private sectors in the field of information systems security.
>
>
>--Has NIST, in the past, established computer security standards that
>industry did not support? Did such standards achieve the results NIST
>desired? What, in your opinion, went wrong with the Clipper initiative?
>
>Answer: Yes! The Digital Signature and the Clipper Standards are prime
>examples of such standards. The 1994 Office of Technology Assessment
>report, "Information Security and Privacy in Network Environments"
>characterized these standards as "...part of a long-term control strategy
>intended to retard the general availability of 'unbreakable' or "hard to
>break' cryptography within the United States, for reasons of national
>security and law enforcement." (p126). I concur with this assessment.

The Clipper Chip entered the market with significant negative factors.
These
include:

     --The design of the chips, and their production and programming were
accomplished by NSA contractors.
     --Any other contractor wishing to participate in the program had to
obtain a SECRET security clearance and obtain an NSA contract.
     --The utilized a classified algorithm that received no open public
scrutiny.
     --The technology could not be implemented in software.
     --Two executive branch agencies served as key escrow holders. Under
the provisions of the escrow policy private sector users could not
obtain
access to their own key in the event of a case of suspected employee
malfeasance.
     --The Clipper chip had virtually no export market because of US
government access to the keys for all devices shipped from the country.

Because of these factors as well as the heavy handed process used to
produce the escrowed encryption standard, the clipper chip was not a

commercial success.

>
>--When NIST developed the Digital Signature Standard did they make full use
>of available commercial standards? In retrospect, and given the fact that
>Federal agencies are now turning to commercially available products, would
>it have been more useful for NIST to adopt a commercially available
>standard at the outset?
>
>Answer: While the RSA algorithm had not been widely recognized in
>the voluntary standards process in 1989, it was clear that it had achieved
>the status of a de facto standard. Throughout the entire process of
>developing the DSS the growing recognition and stature of RSA as the
>commercial standard was apparent to the government.
>
>Adopting RSA would have better served the interests of the taxpayers,
>government users, and the US information technology community. The
>government would be much farther along in using public key technology
>had the adopted a commercially available standard in 1990/1. Rather than
discussing prototypes in 1997, we should be talking about actual
>nationwide, operational digital signature enabled applications involving
>federal
>agencies, private sector entities and individual citizens.

Responses to Congressional Questions--Part II

```
>
>1.  The National Academy of Sciences report released last year entitled
>"Cryptography's role in Securing the Information Society, suggested that
>far more government attention ought to be focused on promoting the use of
>cryptography, particularly in non-confidentiality applications, such as
>user authentication and integrity checks.
>
        o  Do you agree with the National Academy' s conclusion on the need for
>federal efforts to promoted the greater use of cryptography?
>
>Answer:  Yes.  Cryptography is a technology that can significantly enhance
>security and integrity of computer communications and stored data.
>Unfortunately the government has been far more concerned with the potential
>impacts upon intelligence and law enforcement agencies than on addressing
the
>vulnerability created by the lack of cryptographic protection afforded to
>networked information systems.
>
>        o  How should the Department of Commerce serve as an advocate for the
>greater use of encryption technologies in order to underpin the development
>of electronic commerce.
>
>Answer:  The Department of Commerce should seek to aggressively assist the
>civil agencies of the federal government and the private sector apply
>cryptographic technologies.  In accomplishing this objective NIST may have
>to examine how it seeks to accomplish its fundamental mission and move from
>a research oriented program to one that is based upon the application of
>technology developed by the private sector to real world problems.  However
>it is necessary to remind the Committee that NIST must be provided with the
>financial resources to accomplish this important work.  Adequate financial
>resources are necessary to sustain NIST's independence and objectivity in
>the encryption debate.
>
>NIST could also seek to prepare a series of case studies on the successful
>use of cryptography by public and private sector organizations.  These
>could be made available to other organizations seeking to learn from the
>experiences of others.  NIST could also sponsor other conferences and
>meetings focused on promoting the use of cryptography.
>
>        o  Should NIST, for example, provide a central clearinghouse for public
>information on information security threats?
```

>Answer: NIST could provide such a service to government and public sector
>users. Indeed NIST has undertaken to support federal agencies, on a a
>reimbursable basis, through the activities of its Federal Computer
>Emergency Response Center (FEDCERC). However this activity, like so much
>of the NIST security program is constrained by the availability of funds.
>If NIST is to meet the expectations of the Congress, the federal user
>community and the private sector it must be provided with a sustained level
>of funding need to accomplish its important mission. The total disparity
>of funding between NIST and NSA for information systems security should be
>examined by the Committee.
>
>2. What kinds of initiatives could the government take to promote the
>development of a national infrastructure to support commercial and private
>uses of encryption technologies.
>
>Answer: Many potential initiatives have been discussed in answers to other
>questions posed by the Committee. Some of the positive measures for
>promoting the infrastructure for the use of cryptography include:
>
>   --Resolving the legality of the use of cryptographic based digital
>signatures in such federal programs as tax filings, electronic submissions
>to regulatory agencies and federal courts, financial transactions.
>
>   --Resolving issues related to liability with respect to electronic
>contracting, certificate authority operations, etc.
>
>   --Require the use of encryption based signature technologies for
>electronic interactions within the government and between the government
>and the private sector.
>
>   --Separate the issue of digital signature useage and certificate
>authority operation from the issue of key recovery, as mandated in S909.
>
>3A. Is there a federal role concerning the development of uniform
>standards and procedures for certification authorities for digital
>signature?
>
>Answer: Yes. However, it is limited and must be exercised
>with caution. The following are a few of the initiatives that the Federal
>government might consider (or enhance).
>
>   a. Facilitate the development of criteria for the certification of CAs.
>Further collaboration between NIST and private
>enterprise and organizations is needed to move the accreditation process

>forward.
>
>   b. Facilitate the testing and certification of accreditors of CAs
>
>   c. Cooperate with groups such as PKIX and the Information Security
>Committee of the ABA to develop uniform disclosure mechanisms (so that
>notices, warnings, and various other legal and practices materials will
>reliably be presented to PKI users) -- which includes the robust adoption
>and enforcement of X.509 v3 extensions. In fact, such cooperation should
>advance to many international fora with Federal involvement.
>
>
>3B.   Some states have begun to establish a legal framework for a digital
>signature infrastructure; what if any, should be the federal role to
>encourage the development of consistent requirements?
>
>Answer: Advance Federal legislation that preempts inconsistent state
>legislation/regulation (that is draconian, or otherwise creates a burdensome
>on commercial CAs). However, there should first be a meaningful, rigorous
>effort to study the industry and corresponding issues. The government must
involve the CA community in such study. To date, this simply not
>happened. Also . . .
>
>
>   i. Federal legislation should not favor CAs within particular
>vertical markets (such as the financial services industry) because
>doing so will prejudice and unjustly the beneficial development of
>general CAs (such as VeriSign). General CAs require legislative treatment
>no less than any particular vertical markets.

>   ii. Federal legislation should address quality, liability, and
>enforceability issues. There are typically only a few core issues
>included in digital signature legislation -- one is to ensure the quality
>of CAs (by licensure, accreditation or registration), another is to
>assure a fair and certain apportionment of liability (or, even a "safe
>harbor" for CAs that comply with the legislation and the CA's
>certification practice statement), and a third is to ensure the
>enforceability of digitally signed transactions. Note: I believe that
>Federal legislation should not require licensure. Rather, it could
>provide for special benefits to those CAs that undertake voluntary
>accreditation.
>
>
>   iii. Federal legislation should not regulate CAs regarding key
>escrow/key recovery. Instead, any key escrow/recovery legislation

>should be dealt with separately. Requiring CAs to hold, relinquish or
>otherwise undertake key recovery functions that transcend PKI
>certification services diminishes their independence, perceive
>trustworthiness and ultimately their commercial viability.
>
>
>   iv. Federal legislation should recognize and exploit the unique
>technical features and security services of certificate-based digital
>signatures. That is, digital signature legislation should not be
>"technology neutral" but should expressly embrace and facilitate digital
>signatures.
>
>
>   v. Federal legislation should address commercial and consumer
>transactions. It should not be limited to government/public
>sector-related transactions because the real needs are for transactional
>certainty and reasonable ascertainment of liability within the commercial
>marketplace. I anticipate that legislation that is limited to
>government-related transactions (such as the Cal. Digital Signature Act)
>will typically require remedial legislation to accommodate commercial
>transactions in the near future.
>
>
>   vi. Fderal legislation should harmonize with international
>digital signature legislative initiatives such as the current work of the
>United Nations Commission on International Trade Law (UNCITRAL) to
>(hopefully) create model statutory provisions for certification
>authorities. The efforts of the National Conference of
>Commissioners on Uniform State Laws (which only recently began
>considering a digital commerce model law) is most likely too little, to
>late. The best demonstration of the benefit and success to doing so is
>UNCITRAL's Model Law on Electronic Commerce. This Model Law was
>completed by the UN in June '96 and has affected almost every electronic
>commerce law in the world (it has also influenced the VeriSign CPS).
>
>
>4. The bill proposes to expand the role of the Computer System Security
>and Privacy Advisory Board to be a forum for indentifying and seeking
>consensus on computer security, privacy and cryptography issues of public
>concern:
>
>   o Is this a workable approach for improving the communication between
the
>government and the interested public and for arriving at consensus for
>these kinds of issues?

>Answer: The Computer Systems Security and Privacy Advisory Board is an
>underutilized resource that can provide an effective, continuing forum for
>the government to receive advise on emerging information security issues.
>The Board did provide a very useful public service by focusing the
>spotlight of openness on the Clipper Chip proposal. Unfortunately the
>Board has been hampered in the past by several factors. These include: (1)
>The lack of resources. The Board has no dedicated research staff to
>support its work. (2) It has not been allowed to hold public meetings
>outside of the Washington DC area., and (3) The difficulty in getting
>potential members processed for appointment to the Board.
>
>5. What are the principal reasons in your view for NIST's shortcomings in
>carrying out the purposes of the Computer Security Act of 1987?
>
>Answer: There is no single reason, but several factors must be considered
>in addressing the lack of success in implementing the 1987 statue. These
>include a lack of funds, but this can not completely explain the problem.
>I believe that a fundamental issue is that a succession senior Department
>of Commerce officials were not sincerely interested in the computer
>security problem and did not want to provide the leadership needed to make
>the Computer Security Act a success. In addition the responsibility for
>computer security leadership for the civil agencies was given to NIST,
>which considered itself a technical organization and was not prepared to
>become involved in the political, managerial and other non-technical
>aspects of the total computer security problem.
>
>Another aspect of the Computer Security Act problem was the role of the
>National Security Agency and its desire to have a dominant role on all
>aspects of the cryptography problem. In my opinion NSA was not prepared to
>allow NIST to play an independent role with respect to cryptography policy.
> As a result NIST quickly lost credibility by serving as a front for
>various NSA commercial cryptography initiatives that gained no acceptance
>in the commercial market.
>
>6. The criticism has been made that the National Security Agency has
>assumed a more influential role in the implementation of the Computer
>Security Act than was anticipated by the legislation. What are your views
>on the nature and extent of the collaboration that should exist between
>NIST and NSA?
>
>Answer: I believe that there should be a strong working relationship
>between NIST and NSA, but this relationship should be based upon a
>recognition that each agency has a different mission and a different
>constituency to support.

>7. The bill tasks NIST to evaluate cmmercially available security products
>in order to assist agencies in the selection of the most appropriate
>solutions for protection of their computer systems. In his testimony, Mr.
>Walker points out the technical difficulties involved and suggests that may
>not be the best use of NIST's resources, while on the other hand , Mr.
>Bidzos notes that this is an important role for NIST. Would the panelists
>care to expand on their views on this point, since knowledge of the
>capabilities of commercial products would seem to be directly connected to
>promotion of their use?
>
>Answer: NIST does have a program (FIPS 140-1) for evaluating US
>cryptographic products used by federal agencies. This program could be
>adapted for the evaluation of foreign products. Knowledge of the current
>state of the art of foreign encryption products is, or should be an
>important factor in making export control determinations. NIST's
>involvement would assure that some degree of openness, and perhaps
>accountability, is introduced into this process. I would be interested in
>seeing an estimate of the actual costs involved in accomplishing this
>function.
>
>8. All you indicate that NIST did not sufficiently involve the energy and
>productivity of the U.S. computer and communications industries in the area
>or cryptography.
>
>8A. What were the causes of this deficiency and how should it be remedied?
>
>Answer: I believe the fundamental cause of this unfortunate relationship
>was the desire to use the opportunity to establish government cryptographic
>standards as a opportunity and a vehicle to manipulate the domestic market
>place for cryptographic algorithms the government believed would represent
>the least threat to the capabilities of those agencies involved in
>electronic surveillance and communications intelligence. The previously
>mentioned 1994 OTA study supports this view.
>
>Perhaps we are past the era of governmental attempts to control the
>cryptography market place by attempting to control or influence the content
>these products. It is necessary to recognize that the DSS and
>Skipjack/Clipper standards were one component of a larger strategy to
>proliferate the Fortezza card by utilizing the government standards process
>and government procurements to promote a specific encryption product.
>Recent government encryption policy pronouncements reflect a fundamental
>shift from a product based strategy to one based upon key recovery as an
>integral part of the key management infrastructure. Such a strategy
>implies government neutrality with respect to algorithms. Indeed recent

>NIST actions with respect to the potential widening of the algorithms
>covered by the Digital Signature Standard reflect this change in policy
>assumptions.
>
>8B Also, what do you believe has been the impact of the shortcomings of
>NIST?
>Answer: There are several impacts. One has been the unfortunate impact
>upon NIST's reputation and credibility of such standards as Clipper and the
>DSS. Another has been the adverse effects upon the civil agencies of the
>federal government who have had real requirements for the cost effective
>cryptographic solution available in commercial products. The federal
>cryptographic standards process has been an effective barrier to such
>agencies as IRS and SSA in their attempts to modernize and realize the
>savings available through the use of electronic filings and electronic
>commerce.

EPIC
MARC ROTENBERG

Computer Security Enhancement Act of 1997
Additional Questions for the Record

prepared for

COMMITTEE ON SCIENCE
U.S. HOUSE OF REPRESENTATIVES
WASHINGTON, DC 20515

What is your assessment of encryption standard setting efforts outside of the United States? How does this relate to the need for the provisions of HR 1903?

Generally, the approach outside of the United States has been one of allowing the free market to develop voluntarily as many different encryption products as desired. The idea is that by allowing companies to compete in developing new and different products, you encourage innovation and increase the chances of finding a strong standard that will protect data to the greatest degree possible. This in turn bolsters consumer confidence on the Internet.

In terms of how this relates to the provisions of HR 1903, as stated in my testimony to the Committee, I believe that it is essential for the United States to take into account what is happening with encryption in other countries. The reason for this is that the Internet does not operate along geographic boundaries. Other countries and web sites are able to provide encryption to their clients to protect client privacy and encourage Internet business. US citizens should be entitled to the same privacy protection and opportunities to access products and information that the Internet provides. In short, the provisions of HR 1903 which allow for consideration of foreign encryption standards recognize the global nature of the Internet and the need to avoid unnecessary obstacles in the development of new technical standards.

How will HR 1903 benefit users of the Internet or consumers of information technology?

One of Epic's goals is to see increased privacy protection for US Internet users through increased use of encryption domestically. I believe that HR 1903 can help achieve that goal.

As discussed above, examining foreign standards of encryption could eventually lead to a stronger domestic encryption standard which would enhance privacy for US Internet users.

Additionally, by strengthening the Advisory Board's role, increasing the input of private sector companies and stating up front that NIST should be looking at already existing technologies, HR

1903 increases the chances of adopting a strong encryption standard that will do more to protect consumers' privacy

Can you describe for us your experiences as a contributor to the international discussions on cryptography policy at the OECD (Organization for Economic Cooperation and Development Panel on Cryptography Policy) this year?

I served as a member of the expert panel of the OECD established for the purpose of creating an international framework for cryptography policy. I had earlier served as an expert member of the OECD panel which developed the guidelines on information security in 1992.

As a member of the expert panel, I participated in the meetings held in Paris, Washington, and Canberra during 1996, and reviewed the draft proposals and made recommendations to the panel.

I also organized, in cooperation with the Global Internet Liberty Campaign, a forum for the OECD delegates that was held in Paris during September that which provided an opportunity for experts in cryptography, law, and human rights to present views to the representatives of the OECD member nations that might not have otherwise been considered in the development of the OECD policy.

The outcome of the OECD process was the promulgation of an international framework for cryptography policy that favors the open, market-driven development of cryptography products and services, and emphasizes the important value of privacy protection in the design and development of information systems.

What impact will the successful attack on DES have on the standards setting process for computer security?

I believe that the failure of the DES standard illustrates why it is important that technical communication standards for civilian use be developed outside of the military purview of the National Security Agency. This was the original intent of the Computer Security Act of 1987. Despite the CSA, however, NSA played a leading role in developing both the Clipper Chip and the DSS, and classified Clipper's Skipjack algorithm on national security grounds which precluded independent evaluation of the system's strengths.

To avoid repeating past mistakes regarding computer security standards, I hope to see future standards developed by NIST, a civilian agency, in an open and accountable way with input from all relevant parties including government, business, technical specialists, and public interest groups.

Do you think that additional moneys for computer security fellowships and grants will help to improve the nation's security?

Yes. By providing financial incentives for graduate students to pursue issues related to computer security, we are building our national expertise on the issues of encryption and other security measures. New research and new ideas will generate new technologies which will improve security for users of the Internet. This is an investment in the future security of our communications nation's infrastructure.

What in your opinion is needed for NIST to adequately set standards for computer security for the Federal civilian agencies?

First and foremost, NIST must carry out the mandate that was given to them by the Computer Security Act of 1987. Without a clear commitment to the goals set out in the CSA, public concerns will remain about the direction and purpose of NIST standard-setting efforts.

Second, NIST must be given the necessary resources to do its job. Problems have arisen in the past where NIST was dependent on the resources of the NSA to carry out its mandate. The agency should be adequately funded to pursue its work.

Third, NIST must be required to consult with experts and outside parties on the best methods by which to achieve its objectives. HR 1903 goes a long way in this regard by requiring NIST to seek recommendations from its Advisory Board, which in turn has the power to consult with industry and the public.

The Electronic Privacy Information Center, of which you are the Director, is extremely active in the area of privacy rights and first amendment issues among others. Can you describe for us what significance if any the Computer Security Enhancement Act of 1997 has on these issues.

Encryption is the critical technology to protect privacy in the information age. While it is not necessarily the case that every implementation of an encryption technique provides greater privacy, it is clear that encryption as one of the building blocks for information privacy and the critical technique for the development of privacy enhancing technologies. By encouraging the development and adoption of strong, robust, encryption standards, the CSEA will promote the development of better methods to protect privacy.

Encryption will also play an important role in the development of a robust and open market for information and ideas in the twenty-first century. Techniques will be established to protect the copyright interests of authors and encourage the publication of new digital works. Encryption techniques will also make possible the protection of anonymous speech, a cherished First Amendment freedom upheld by the Supreme Court as recently as 1995.

Encryption also plays an important role in helping to secure the information infrastructure and thereby helps provide a more stable communications, economic, and political environment for debate and discussion about social matters. In the absence of good techniques to provide infrastructure security, the ability of individuals to exercise political rights may be jeopardized.

What is your opinion of NIST's current standards setting process for computer security? What will the Computer Security Enhancement Act of 1997 do to improve this process?

The current standard-setting process suffers from a credibility problem. Decisions are made without adequate input or accountability. For example, FIPS 185 the Escrowed Encryption Standard went forward over the nearly unanimous option of the user community that responded the Department's request for comment. The CSEA will make the standard-setting process more open, more accountable, and more competitive. This will benefit federal agencies, US firms, and users of new information services.

Your testimony on section 7 of the Computer Security Enhancement Act of 1997 was very favorable. Do you have any addition thoughts on section 7 which you care to share with us?

Since the time of the hearing, it has become increasingly clear that foreign government do not intend to impose the type of controls on the development of encryption that are now under consideration in the United States. At the meeting of the Ministers of the European Commission in Bonn in early July, the leaders of Europe reaffirmed their commitment to the widespread availability of strong encryption to protect the rights of citizens and to promote the development of electronic commerce.

Whatever one's views on the desirability of promoting strong encryption products in the United States -- and my view is clearly that this should be promoted -- it makes little sense to ignore the developments in other countries, particularly given the nature of the Internet and global commerce. Section 7 brings some sanity to policy-making process by requiring consideration of developments outside of the US.

What does the Computer Security Enhancement Act of 1997 do to improve national security?

The development of techniques to protect the security of the nation's infrastructure is a critical objective for national security. The President has recognized that many of our key infrastructures are at risk and that steps must be taken to make our country less vulnerable to risks that result from our growing dependency on advanced communication technologies.

Encryption is the basis for promoting solutions to the problem of network vulnerability. This point has been made by parties on all sides in the encryption debate. Without strong encryption, we will not have strong, secure, robust networks.

CSEA encourages the development of these techniques, as well as broader support for computer security across the federal government. While other threats to national security will remain, the CSEA helps to reduce our exposure in one the areas of greatest vulnerability and most pressing national concern.

What do you believe would be the result of a Federal policy that divests NIST of its jurisdiction and give these duties to National Security Agency?

I believe that this would reduce business and user confidence in the federal government and possibly jeopardize the mission of the National Security Agency. Our experience with both events leading up to the Computer Security Act of 1987 and since passage of the law is that openness, accountability, and private sector input are critical to the development of technical standards and procedures that instill confidence and trust. The NSA's attempt to establish the Clipper standard was a mistake not only because it had severe implications for the privacy rights of all Americans, but also because it ultimately reduced the level of public trust in the technical work of the government. We cannot develop good solutions to difficult problems in an environment characterized by secrecy and little public input. For the NSA, whose mission often requires secrecy, to take on a task that by its nature affects millions of Americans both in and out of government would be to repeat the mistake of Clipper many times over.

Has NIST, in the past, established computer security standards that industry did not support? Did such standards achieve the results NIST desired? What, in your opinion, went wrong with the Clipper initiative?

Both the Digital Signature Standard and the Escrowed Encryption Standard were widely opposed by the user community. More robust products were available from the private sector that offered stronger security and better privacy protection. NIST has had a difficult time to encouraging adoption of these standards and has slowed the process of putting in place necessary security measures.

Regarding Clipper, as I indicated above, there problems both in the effort to establish a technical standard that was such an affront to widely recognized privacy interests as well as the attempt to force a secret, untested technical standard on the user community. Users simply will not trust products that result from such secretive procedures for good reason -- science and innovation require the open exchange of information, the continually testing of ideas, and the constant search for new and better ways to solve problems. It was therefore not a great surprise when a well known cryptographer was able to bust the Clipper algorithm.

Open markets, open research, and open standard-setting are all critical for the successful development of strong, trusted security methods.

When NIST developed the Digital Signature Standard did they make full use of available commercial standards? In retrospect, and given the fact that Federal agencies are now turning to commercially available products, would it have been more useful for NIST to adopt a commercially available standard at the outset?

It is clearly the case that NIST ignored the availability of good commercial software, such as RSA, when it went forward with the DSS. Of great concern is that one of NIST's own scientists expressed the view that the RSA algorithm would be preferable to the standard that was being urged on the agency by the National Security Agency. The selection of the DSS meant that better techniques for privacy and security, developed by US firms for use by US federal agencies, businesses, and computer users, were not made available. CSEA would help prevent such mistakes in the future.

MARC ROTENBERG
Computer Security
Enhancement Act of 1997

Additional Questions for the Record

COMMITTEE ON SCIENCE

U.S. HOUSE OF
REPRESENTATIVES
WASHINGTON, DC 20515

Responses to questions
submitted for the record
byThe Hon. Bart Gordon, (D-TN)

Ranking Member Subcommittee on Technology Committee on Science

1) Certainly, the Federal government must make sure that the most advanced and robust
encryption technology is used in their own computer systems, where a vast amount of
personal information is stored. Federal efforts to promote the
greater use of encryption technology, however, must be part of a
broader, more comprehensive, and forward-looking encryption policy.
Such a policy must emphasize open government procedures, active public
input, and the participation of the best technical experts.

The promise of electronic commerce requires a reliable and secure underlying electronic
transaction system, built on the best available cryptographic
technology. The Department of Commerce should take a strong stance on
private sector leadership and public input on security related policy
and product development, to ensure the rapid and efficient
technological development of such a system.

It is conceivable that at some point in the future NIST could play a role in responding to public concerns about information security threats. But at this point in time I believe that NIST's efforts would be better directed toward security
threats within the federal government.

2)

The government should support effective and greater use of cryptographic technology by promoting its efficient and rapid development. As the CSA recognized, it is critically important that security standards and products be
developed that are compatible with the needs of civilian agencies
within the Federal government and of commercial development in the
private sector.

The government should emphasize private sector collaboration and free science, should enhance openness and public accountability in the development of product, policy and procedures, and should not be improperly influenced by
misplaced national security concerns in the development of information
security technology. >

There are currently many projects underway in the federal government to test the viability of key escrow and key recovery techniques. I believe that the long term interests of privacy protection and online commerce would be better
served if some of theses efforts were redirected toward the promotion
of techniques for anonymous transactions. Such efforts are currently
underway in several countries and will play an important role in
developing the techniques that are necessary for privacy protection in
advanced digital networks.

3)

I have no strong opinion as to the appropriate role of the federal government in the development of uniform standards for digital signatures. I do think it will be important to consider a wider range of ethical, legal, and social
issues than are current contemplated in the debate over digital
signatures. This would include, for example, the role of personal
identification in non-commercial relations, the implications for
privacy of universal identification schemes, and the consequences for
personal freedom where digital signatures are based on biometric
identifiers

4)

The Computer System Security and Privacy Advisory Board (CSSPAB) has done
excellent work since passage of the Computer Security Act of 1987. CSSPAB provides
the critical conduit between the Commerce Department and the public on matters
concerning security and privacy within the federal government.
The CSSPAB also provides a high level of expertise and review for the
policy-making process. The Advisory Board provides a solid foundation
for future work between the government and the interested parties. The
CSEA wisely builds on the good record of the Advisory
Board.

5)

NIST's shortcomings in carrying out its statutory mandate to implement the CSA was the
result of a combination of factors, most important of which were a lack of
resources, and an unfortunate reliance (perhaps as a result of NIST's
lack of resources) on the National Security Agency in the development
of technical standards. NSA's emphasis on national security resulted
in an exclusion of private sector participation, diminished public
accountability and resulted in more secrecy as NIST developed its
computer security policy and procedures.

6)

While NIST should be allowed to collaborate with the NSA and draw upon its technical
resources, it is crucial that NIST cooperate with the private sector in
the development of technical standards. Such participation will
provide for critical external, non-governmental perspective on policy,
and will inject positive and dynamic energy from the scientific
community and the computer industry in the development of computer
security systems. The CSEA makes clear that NIST's reliance on NSA
guidelines be permissive, rather than mandatory. This will help ensure
that NIST does not continue to be improperly swayed from its important
and critical mandate in this area. NSA concerns regarding classified
information should not be imposed on NIST's mandate of protecting
"unclassified, but sensitive" information.

7)

Mr. Gordon, you are correct that knowledge of the capabilities of commercial products is
directly connected to the promotion of their use and critical for NIST
to make fully informed recommendations to safeguard the security of
government information systems. NIST has in the past ignored

commercial products that could have satisfied agency requirements. This
happened, for example, in the selection of the algorithm for the
Digital Signature Standard. The CSEA correctly requires NIST to
consider these options in th development of recommendations for sec
products.

8)

The problem of private sector exclusion from NIST's procedures and policies emerged as
the result of the Memorandum of Understanding that was signed in 1989. NSA's
misplaced emphasis on national security resulted in an exclusion
of private sector participation, diminished public accountability and
resulted in more secrecy as NIST developed its computer security
policy. NSA-imposed restrictions stifled innovation, and deprived NIST
of the benefits of the vigorous research and development that goes on
the academic community, and in the private computer
industry.

The impact of this shortcoming of NIST is best illustrated by the problems with the
development of the Digital Signature Standard (DSS), which is widely
criticized as a flawed standard, and one that is inferior to those
developed in the private sector. In short, the DSS experience
illustrates that the lack of private sector participation resulted in
the development of a substandard technology. The best way to remedy
this shortcoming is to promote rapid and open development of
technology, by ensuring collaborative efforts between the government
agencies and private industry. The Computer Security Enhancement Act
goes a long way in encouraging the use of existing private sector
technologies, and the development of new collaborative standards and
technologies, and in this way attempts to remedy NIST's past
deficiencies in promoting private sector initiative and
participation.

ISBN 0-16-058582-4

APEX
TP_CF
9780160558825

76523826—17